No-Bake
Cookies

Also by Camilla V. Saulsbury

Cookie Dough Delights

Brownie Mix Bliss

Cake Mix Cookies

No-Bake
Cookies

More Than 150 Fun, Easy, & Delicious Recipes for Cookies, Bars, and Other Cool Treats Made Without Baking

Camilla V. Saulsbury

CUMBERLAND HOUSE

No-Bake Cookies
Published by Cumberland House Publishing, Inc., an imprint of Sourcebooks, Inc.
PO Box 4410
Naperville, IL 60567-4410
www.sourcebooks.com

Cover design: JulesRules Design
Text design: Lisa Taylor

Library of Congress Cataloging-in-Publication Data

Saulsbury, Camilla V.
  No-bake cookies : more than 150 fun, easy, & delicious recipes for cookies, bars, and other cool treats made without baking / Camilla V. Saulsbury.
     p. cm.
  Includes index.
  1. Cookies. I. Title.
  TX772.S2585 2006
  641.8'654—dc22

                                                                    2006009850

Printed in the United States of America
POD 10 9 8 7 6 5 4 3

To Nicholas

Contents

Acknowledgments

So many people deserve thanks for every stage of this book. For support and love: Kevin, for everything, every day; Charlotte and Daniel, parents extraordinaire; Sean, Becca, and Robin, wonderful friends as much as siblings; Kenji and Hugh, for inspiration and for keeping me silly; Mindy, Tatiana, Abby, and Sara, for being the best girlfriends; and Lindsey, Liz, and Kirsten, for doing so much, without even realizing it.

Heaps of thanks to all of the dedicated, talented, and extremely hard-working people at Cumberland, especially Ron, Julie, Lisa, and Tracy. Could I be any luckier?

And finally, to Nicholas, for giving me perspective and making it all worthwhile.

No-Bake Cookies

Introduction

Big, splurge-worthy flavors. Little effort. Readily available ingredients. Terrific results, time and again. These are the principles behind *No-Bake Cookies*.

If you love making cookies as much as I do, you may be pleased to learn that you can make some of the best cookies and bars around without ever turning on the oven. It may sound surprising, but there's no magic involved. Just a few time-honored techniques for producing irresistible treats while both you and the kitchen remain cool.

With a host of basic building blocks (e.g., an assortment of cereals, crushed graham crackers, cookie crumbs, butter, nut butters, cream cheese, and chocolate) and a heap of delicious flavor options (e.g., dried fruits, nuts, toffee, coffee, vanilla, spices, and more), no-bake cookies are literally a matter of minutes in the making.

The recipes in this collection are a boon for busy home cooks with a penchant for sweet treats—they come together quickly with readily available ingredients and a few straightforward steps. Perfect for the warmer months, cookie cravings can be satisfied with an easy batch of icebox bars, simple drop cookies, or a multitude of deep chocolate delights.

No-bake cookies make great "first time" cooking fun for kids, too. Even the youngest of children can help with the measuring and stirring of many of these easy options while Mom, Dad, or big brother handle more advanced elements of the process like chopping nuts and melting butter on the stovetop.

And it's very likely you're already an experienced no-bake cookie maker. Rice crispy treats, chocolate-oatmeal no-bakes, peanut butter bars—a short list of no-bake cookies are already part of your repertoire. With *No-Bake Cookies*, you can expand that list exponentially.

Think Maple Praline Drop Cookies. S'mores Clusters. Quick Caramel Delightfuls. Mixed Fruit, Seed & Nut Energy Bars. PB & J Bites. Maui-Wowie Macadamia

Bars. Irish Cream Mousse Bars. Key Lime Squares. Butterscotch Pudding Bars. Blackberry Mascarpone Bars. These represent the mere tip of the iceberg.

So whether you're looking for a fun-time treat for the kids, a healthy snack for the lunchbox, a dreamy chocolate indulgence, or a creamy-cool summery icebox bar, a recipe from the *No-Bake Cookies* cookbook surely fits the bill.

I hope you will join me in the delectable fun of no-bake cookies. Make a pot of tea or a big, frothy cappuccino, take a moment to relax, and then pore over these pages. I'm confident you'll find many delicious and inspiring recipes that you can soon call your own.

NO-BAKE COOKIE PREP

In general, no-bake cookies require far less preparation than traditional baked cookies. Nevertheless, it's worth taking some care before beginning to ensure excellent and consistent results, time and again.

• Read the recipe thoroughly. Note the required ingredients and equipment needed as well as any chilling and cooling times.
• Gather the necessary ingredients, checking for freshness (see the "No-Bake Cookie Pantry" section that follows for tips on how to do so).
• Gather the necessary equipment, including mixing bowls, wooden spoons, and wax paper.
• Prep the ingredients as needed, such as chopping nuts, zesting lemons, softening cream cheese, or melting butter.
• Prepare any baking pans or cookie sheets as specified in the recipe. Many of the no-bake cookies in this collection set up fairly quickly; hence it is important for sheets and pans to be ready for making cookie drops or pressing cookie bars into shape. If no advanced preparation is needed, set the pan or sheet aside so that it is ready to be used when needed.
• Reread the recipe.
• Precisely measure all of the ingredients. No-bake cookies are less dependent on the precision measuring required for oven baking, but accuracy is still important for achieving optimal results each time. See the "Measuring Ingredients" section on page 10 for tips on measuring dry, liquid, and moist ingredients.
• Mix ingredients according to recipe specifications.
• Use a reliable kitchen timer when timing is specified in the recipe. This allows for precision stovetop cooking and successful chilling.

THE NO-BAKE COOKIE PANTRY

Cereals: A variety of ready-to-eat cereals are used throughout this book, including crisp rice cereal, cornflakes, wheat and barley nuggets (e.g., Grape Nuts), graham cracker cereal, and crisp honey-nut flakes and clusters cereal. Both name-brand and store-brand cereals were used to test recipes in this collection; either variety may be used. Use only fresh, crisp cereal for best results.

Oats: Two types of oats are used throughout this collection, old-fashioned and quick-cooking oats. Old-fashioned oats are rolled and are made from the entire oat kernel. With quick-cooking oats the oat kernel is cut into pieces before being rolled thinly. Use the oats specified in the recipe for best results. Avoid using instant oatmeal, which consists of oats that have been very finely cut and processed. Store oats in a cool, dry place in a tightly covered container for up to six months. Oats may also be frozen in a zip-top plastic freezer bag for up to one year. Oats do not spoil but may become stale with age.

Cookie Crumbs: A variety of store-bought cookies are used in crushed and crumbled form throughout this collection. Both name-brand and store-brand cookies were used to test recipes in this collection; either variety may be used. Use only fresh, crisp cookies for best results.

Graham Crackers: Both whole graham crackers and graham cracker crumbs are used throughout this collection. Graham crackers are rectangular-shaped, whole wheat crackers that have been lightly sweetened. Use only fresh, crisp graham crackers for best results. Where graham cracker crumbs are specified in a recipe, ready-made graham cracker crumbs may be used. Look for them in the baking section of the grocery store where flour is shelved.

Butter: Butter is used in many of the recipes throughout this collection to bolster the flavor of the cookies and bars. Fresh butter should have a delicate cream flavor and pale yellow color. Butter quickly picks up off-flavors during storage and when exposed to oxygen; once the carton is opened, place it in a zipper-top plastic food bag or airtight container. Store it away from foods with strong odors, especially items such as onions or garlic.

Melted butter is used in many recipes throughout this book. For best results, cut the specified amount of butter into small pieces, place in a small saucepan, and allow to melt over the lowest heat setting of the burner. Once the butter has melted, remove pan from heat and cool. To speed the cooling pour the melted butter into a small bowl or liquid measuring cup.

Softened butter is also required in several recipes throughout this collection. The easiest method for softening butter is to remove from the refrigerator the amount needed for the recipe. Let it stand 30–45 minutes at room temperature. Cutting the butter into small chunks will reduce the softening time to about 15 minutes. If time is really limited, try grating the cold butter on the large holes of a cheese grater. The small bits of butter will be soft in just a few minutes. Alternatively, place the cold butter between sheets of wax paper and hit it several times with a rolling pin (this also works as great stress relief!). Avoid softening butter in the microwave. It will typically melt at least part of the butter, even if you watch it closely.

Chocolate: Two general types of chocolate are used throughout this collection. The first type is chocolate chips, available in semisweet, milk, white, and miniature semisweet. Some premium brands offer bittersweet chocolate chips, which may be used interchangeably with semisweet chocolate chips. The second general type of chocolate is baking chocolate, which is typically available in 6- or 8-ounce packages with the chocolate most often individually wrapped in 1-ounce squares or occasionally in 2-ounce bars. It is available in unsweetened, bittersweet, semisweet, milk, and white chocolate varieties.

Store both chocolate chips and baking chocolate in a dry, cool place between 60° and 78°. Wrapping chocolate in moisture-proof wrap or in a zip-lock plastic bag is a good idea if the temperature is higher or the humidity is above 50 percent. Chocolate can also be stored in the fridge, but let it stand at room temperature before using.

If the chocolate from your pantry has a white, crusty-looking film on it, don't toss it. This is commonly called "bloom" and develops when the chocolate is exposed to varying temperatures, from hot to cold. The change in heat allows the cocoa butter to melt and rise to the surface of the chocolate. Bloom does not affect the quality or flavor of the chocolate. The chocolate will look normal again once it is melted or used in baking.

Cream Cheese: All of the recipes in this book use "brick"-style cream cheese, which is typically packaged in 3- or 8-ounce rectangular packages. Avoid using soft-spread, flavored, or whipped cream cheese to achieve the best results.

To soften cream cheese, unwrap it and cut it into chunks with a sharp knife. Let it stand at room temperature 30–45 minutes until softened. For speed softening, place the chunks of cream cheese on a microwavable plate or in a microwavable bowl and microwave on high for 15 seconds. If necessary, microwave 5–10 seconds longer.

Eggs: Use large eggs in all of the recipes in this book. Select clean, fresh eggs which have been handled properly and refrigerated. Do not use dirty, cracked, or leaking eggs that may have a bad odor or unnatural color when cracked open. They may have become contaminated with harmful bacteria such as salmonella. Cold eggs are easiest to separate; eggs at room temperature beat to high volume.

Eggs may be checked for freshness by filling a deep bowl with enough cold water to cover an egg. Place the egg in the water. If the egg lies on its side on the bottom of the bowl, it is fresh. If the egg stands up and bobs on the bottom, it isn't quite as fresh but is still acceptable for baking. If the egg floats on the surface, it should be discarded.

Margarine: Margarine may be substituted for butter, but it is not recommended because it lacks the rich flavor that butter offers. However, if using margarine in place of butter, it is essential that it is a 100 percent vegetable oil, solid stick. Margarine spreads—in tub or stick form—will alter the liquid and fat combination of the recipe, leading to either unsatisfactory or downright disastrous results. You can determine the fat percentage in one of two ways. In some cases, the percentage is printed on the box. If it reads anything less than 100 percent oil, it is a spread and should be avoided. If the percentage is not printed on the outside of the box, flip it over and check the calories. If it is 100 calories per tablespoon, it is 100 percent vegetable oil; any less, and it is less than 100 percent and should not be used.

Nonstick Cooking Spray: Nonstick cooking spray is canned oil that has been packed under pressure and is dispersed by a propellant. It is flavorless, coats pans evenly, and allows for easier removal of the cooled and chilled bars throughout this collection.

Vanilla Extract: Vanilla extract adds a sweet, fragrant flavor to no-bake cookies and is particularly good for enhancing the flavor of chocolate. It is produced by extracting the flavor of dried vanilla beans with an alcohol and water mixture. It is then aged for several months. The three most common types of beans used to make vanilla extract are Bourbon-Madagascar, Mexican, and Tahitian.

Store vanilla extract in a cool, dark place, with the bottle tightly closed to prevent it from evaporating and losing flavor. It will stay fresh for about two years unopened and for one year after being opened.

Imitation vanilla flavoring can be substituted for vanilla extract, but it may have a slight or prominent artificial taste, depending on the brand. It is about half the cost of real vanilla extract; however, it's worth the extra expense of splurging on the real thing.

Shelled nuts: Use plain, unsalted nuts unless specified otherwise in the recipe. To determine whether shelled nuts are fresh, taste them: they should taste and smell fresh, not rancid with an off-flavor. Frozen nuts are prone to freezer burn if stored improperly and may taste old or stale. Shelled nuts should also have a crisp texture, should be relatively uniform in color, and should not be shriveled or discolored in spots.

Toasting nuts before adding them to a recipe can greatly intensify their flavor and hence their contribution to a recipe. To toast without turning on the oven, place them in an ungreased skillet over medium heat (3–4 minutes), stirring frequently, until golden brown (note that this method works best with chopped, as opposed to whole, nuts).

Coconut: To toast, place the coconut in a large, heavy skillet set over medium heat. Cook and stir constantly with a wooden spoon or spatula until a deep golden brown, about 2–3 minutes. Immediately transfer coconut to a plate or dish to cool (it will burn if left in the pan). Cool completely before adding to the recipe.

Spices: All of the recipes in this book use ground, as opposed to whole, spices. Freshness is everything with ground spices. The best way to determine if a ground spice is fresh is to open the container and smell it. If it still has a strong fragrance, it is still acceptable for use. If not, toss it and make a new purchase.

Peanut Butter: Peanut butter is a spreadable blend of ground peanuts, vegetable oil, and salt. Two types of peanut butter are used throughout this collection: creamy and chunky. Avoid using natural or old-fashioned peanut butter in all of the recipes in this book because the consistency is significantly different from the commercial styles of peanut butter.

Marshmallows and Marshmallow Creme: Marshmallows are white, spongy, pillow-shaped confections made from sugar, corn syrup, gelatin, and egg whites.

They are available ready-made in both large and miniature sizes. Opened packages of marshmallows should be placed in a large, zip-top plastic bag to preserve their freshness. Marshmallow creme (also called marshmallow fluff) is available in jar form and looks like melted marshmallow.

Granulated White Sugar: Granulated white sugar is the most common sweetener used throughout this collection. It is refined cane or beet sugar. If a recipe in the book calls for sugar without specifying which one, use granulated white sugar. Once opened, store granulated sugar in an airtight container in a cool, dry place.

Brown Sugar: Brown sugar is granulated sugar that has some molasses added to it. The molasses gives the brown sugar a soft texture. Light brown sugar has less molasses and a more delicate flavor than dark brown sugar. If a recipe in the book calls for brown sugar without specifying which one, use light brown sugar. If you are out of brown sugar, substitute 1 cup granulated white sugar plus 2 tablespoons molasses for each cup of brown sugar. Once opened, store brown sugar in an airtight container or zip-top plastic bag to prevent clumping.

Powdered Sugar: Powdered sugar (also called confectioner's sugar) is granulated sugar that has been ground to a fine powder. Cornstarch is added to prevent the sugar from clumping together. It is used in recipes where regular sugar would be too grainy. If you are out of powdered sugar, place 1 cup granulated white sugar plus $1/8$ teaspoon cornstarch in a food processor or blender, then process on high speed until finely powdered. Once opened, store powdered sugar in an airtight container or zip-top plastic bag to prevent clumping.

Corn Syrup: Corn syrup is a thick, sweet syrup made by processing cornstarch with acids or enzymes. Light corn syrup is further treated to remove any color. Light corn syrup is very sweet but does not have much flavor. Dark corn syrup has coloring and flavoring added to make it caramel-like. Unopened containers of corn syrup may be stored at room temperature. After opening, store corn syrup in the refrigerator to protect against mold.

Corn syrup will keep indefinitely when stored properly.

Honey: Honey is the nectar of plants that has been gathered and concentrated by honey bees. Any variety of honey may be used in the recipes throughout this collection. Unopened containers of honey may be stored at room temperature. After opening, store honey in the refrigerator to protect against mold. Honey will keep indefinitely when stored properly.

Maple Syrup: Maple syrup is a thick, liquid sweetener made by boiling the sap from maple trees. Maple syrup has a strong, pure maple flavor. Maple-flavored pancake syrup is not recommended as a substitute for pure maple syrup as it is corn syrup with coloring and artificial maple flavoring added. Unopened containers of maple syrup may be stored at room temperature. After opening, store maple syrup in the refrigerator to protect against mold. Maple syrup will keep indefinitely when stored properly.

Molasses: Molasses is made from the juice of sugar cane or sugar beets that is boiled until a syrupy mixture remains. Light molasses is lighter in flavor and color and results from the first boiling of the syrup. Dark molasses, dark in both flavor and color, is not as sweet as light molasses. It comes from the second boiling of the syrup. Light and dark molasses may be used interchangeably in the recipes in this collection. Blackstrap molasses is thick, very dark, and has a bitter flavor; it is not recommended for the recipes in this collection. Unopened containers of molasses may be stored at room temperature. After opening, store molasses in the refrigerator to protect against mold. Molasses will keep indefinitely when stored properly.

MEASURING INGREDIENTS

Measuring Dry Ingredients: When measuring a dry ingredient such as sugar, spices, or salt, spoon it into the appropriate-size dry measuring cup or measuring spoon, heaping it up over the top. Next, slide a straight-edged utensil, such as a knife, across the top to level off the extra. Be careful not to shake or tap the cup or spoon to settle the ingredient or you will have more than you need.

Measuring Liquid Ingredients: Use a clear plastic or glass measuring cup or container with lines up the sides to measure liquid ingredients. Set the container on the counter and pour the liquid to the appropriate mark. Lower your head to read the measurement at eye level.

Measuring Syrups, Honey, and Molasses: Measure syrups, honey, and molasses as you would other liquid ingredients, but lightly spray the measuring cup or container with nonstick cooking spray before filling. The syrup, honey, or molasses will slide out of the cup without sticking, allowing for both accurate measuring and easy cleanup.

Measuring Moist Ingredients: Some moist ingredients, such as brown sugar, coconut, and dried fruits, must be firmly packed into the measuring cup to be measured accurately. Use a dry measuring cup for these ingredients. Fill the measuring cup to slightly overflowing, then pack down the ingredient firmly with the back of a spoon. Add more of the ingredient and pack down again until the cup is full and even with the top of the measure.

Measuring Butter: Butter is typically packaged in stick form with markings on the wrapper indicating tablespoon and cup measurements. Use a sharp knife to cut off the amount needed for a recipe.

$1/4$ cup = $1/2$ stick = 4 tablespoons = 2 ounces
$1/2$ cup = 1 stick = $1/4$ pound = 4 ounces
1 cup = 2 sticks = $1/2$ pound = 8 ounces
2 cups = 4 sticks = 1 pound = 16 ounces

Measuring Cream Cheese: Like sticks of butter, bricks of cream cheese are typically packaged with markings on the wrapper indicating tablespoon and cup measurements. Use a sharp knife to cut off the amount needed for a recipe.

Measuring Spices, Salt, Baking Powder, & Baking Soda: Use the standard measuring spoon size specified in the recipe and be sure the spoon is dry when measuring. Fill a standard measuring spoon to the top and level with a spatula or knife. When a recipe calls for a dash of a spice or salt, use about $1/16$ of a teaspoon. A pinch is considered to be the amount of salt that can be held between the tips of the thumb and forefinger, and is also approximately $1/16$ of a teaspoon.

Measuring Nuts: Spoon nuts into a dry measuring cup to the top. Four ounces of nuts is the equivalent of 1 cup chopped nuts.

Measuring Extracts & Flavorings: Fill the standard measuring spoon size specified in the recipe to the top, being careful not to let any spill over. It's a good idea to avoid measuring extracts or flavorings over the mixing bowl because the spillover will go into the bowl and you will not know the amount of extract or flavoring you have added.

COOLING & SERVING

Cooling: Cooling directions vary for no-bake cookies. Most drop and shaped no-bake cookies must be formed immediately before the cookie mixture hardens. Similarly, cereal bars must be pressed into the appropriate-sized pan while the mixture is still warm and pliable. Most no-bake cookies are ready to be eaten as soon as they cool. Several no-bake bar cookies need to be cut before completely cooled, so be sure to read the recipe in its entirety before beginning the recipe.

Cutting Bar Cookies: Cut cooled no-bake bars with a hard plastic or table knife to ensure smooth-sided bars. For precision cutting, use a pastry scraper.

A hot knife will cut no-bake bar cookies even more easily. Simply dip the sharp knife in hot water, wipe with a dry kitchen towel, then make a cut. After each cut, clean and reheat the knife by dipping it in hot water and wiping with a paper towel before resuming.

Aluminum Foil (Foil-Lining Pans): Lining baking pans with aluminum foil is a great way to cut no-bake bars more easily. When a pan is foil-lined, it is easy to remove the entire batch of bars from the pan at once, making the cutting of perfectly uniform squares and bars a snap. When the bars are cooled or chilled until set, lift them out of the pan, peel back the foil, and cut. Foil-lining also makes cleaning up easy.

Foil-lining is simple. Begin by turning the pan upside down. Tear off a piece of aluminum foil longer than the pan and shape the foil over the pan. Carefully remove the foil and set aside. Flip the pan over and gently fit the shaped foil into the pan, allowing the foil to hang over the sides (the overhang ends will work as "handles" when the brownies or bars are removed).

STORAGE

General Storage: Store no-bake bars and cookies in an airtight container at room temperature for optimal freshness, unless specified otherwise in the recipe. Sturdier bars and cookies can be placed in a ziplock plastic bag; more delicate varieties are better off stacked between layers of wax paper in a plastic container. Bar cookies can be stacked in a container between layers of wax paper or stored in their baking pan. Cover the top tightly with aluminum foil, plastic wrap, or a lid.

EQUIPMENT

No-Bake Cookie Equipment Checklist:

✓ 13x9x2-inch plain aluminum rectangular pan

✓ 15x10x1-inch jelly roll pan

✓ 9x9x2-inch square baking pan

✓ 8x8x2-inch square baking pan

✓ Plain aluminum cookie sheets (at least two)

✓ Aluminum foil

✓ Plastic wrap

✓ Wax paper

✓ Dry measuring cups in graduated sizes $1/4$, $1/3$, $1/2$, and 1 cup

✓ Liquid measuring cup (preferably clear glass or plastic)

✓ Measuring spoons in graduated sizes $1/8$, $1/4$, $1/2$, and 1 teaspoon as well as 1 tablespoon

✓ Wooden spoon(s)

✓ Mixing bowls (at least one each of small, medium, and large sizes)

✓ Rubber or silicone spatula (for scraping the sides of a mixing bowl)

✓ Metal spatula or pancake turner for removing no-bake bars from pans (use a plastic spatula if you are using a nonstick-coated cookie sheet or baking pan)

✓ Wire cooling racks

✓ Oven mitts or holders (for holding hot saucepans and skillets)

✓ Kitchen timer

✓ Cutting board(s)

✓ Rolling pin or mallet (for crushing cookies, graham crackers, and candies)

✓ Wire whisk

✓ Chef's knife

✓ Kitchen spoons (everyday place setting soup and teaspoons for drop cookies)

✓ Small off-set metal spatula (ideal for frosting both cookies and bars)

✓ Metal pastry scraper (the perfect tool for cutting bars into perfect squares and bars)

✓ Cookie scoops (look like small ice cream scoops—use for perfectly measured drop cookies)

✓ Food processor

✓ Zester

Drop Cookies

Chocolate-Chip Peanut Butter Cookies

Your only dilemma with these cookies will be deciding with whom to share them.

1	**cup creamy peanut butter**
1	**cup powdered sugar**
$^1/_2$	**cup milk**
2	**teaspoons vanilla extract**
2	**cups quick-cooking oats, uncooked**
2	**cups semisweet chocolate chips**

❖ Line cookie sheets with wax paper.

❖ In a large bowl stir together the peanut butter, powdered sugar, milk, and vanilla with a wooden spoon, mixing until well blended. Stir in oats and chocolate chips.

❖ Drop by kitchen teaspoonfuls onto wax-paper-lined sheets. Store tightly covered in an airtight container between layers of wax paper. ❖ Makes about 48 cookies.

Drop Cookies

Maple Praline Cookies

The taste of fall, all wrapped up in a heavenly cookie, is deceptively easy to pre-pare. To increase the autumnal experience, add $^1/_2$ cup chopped dried cran-berries to the mix along with the oats.

$1^1/_4$	cups maple syrup
$^1/_4$	cup light corn syrup
$^1/_4$	cup ($^1/_2$ stick) butter
1	cup chopped pecans
1	teaspoon vanilla extract
3	cups quick-cooking oats, uncooked

◇ Line cookie sheets with wax paper.

◇ In a large saucepan combine the maple syrup and corn syrup. Bring to a boil over medium heat, stirring frequently. Continue boiling 3 minutes, stirring frequently.

◇ Remove from heat. Stir in butter until melted. Stir in the pecans, vanilla, and oats. Working quickly, drop by tablespoonfuls onto wax-paper-lined sheets. Let stand until firm. Store tightly covered. ◇ Makes about 36 cookies.

Drop Cookies

Chocolate Oatmeal No-Bakes

Cocoa, butter, and oats make for a dandy of a chocolate cookie. Once these treats set up, they have a rich, fudge-y taste and consistency.

2	cups packed light brown sugar
$^1/_2$	cup (1 stick) butter
$^1/_2$	cup canned evaporated milk
$^1/_3$	cup unsweetened cocoa powder
1	teaspoon vanilla extract
3	cups quick-cooking oats, uncooked

◆ Line cookie sheets with wax paper.

◆ In a large saucepan combine the brown sugar, butter, evaporated milk, and cocoa powder. Bring to a boil over medium heat, stirring frequently. Continue boiling 3 minutes, stirring frequently.

◆ Remove from heat and stir in the vanilla and oats. Working quickly, drop by tablespoonfuls onto wax-paper-lined sheets. Let stand until firm. Store tightly covered. ◆ Makes about 36 cookies.

Drop Cookies

White Chocolate, Coconut, & Lime Cookies

Both coconut and lime lovers will delight in these drops, rich in the flavors of the tropics.

1	cup white chocolate chips
5	tablespoons butter
16	large marshmallows
1	tablespoon fresh lime juice
2	teaspoons grated lime zest
1	teaspoon ground ginger
2	cups quick-cooking oats, uncooked
1	cup sweetened flake coconut

◆ Line cookie sheets with wax paper.

◆ In a large saucepan melt the white chocolate chips with the butter, marshmallows, and lime juice over low heat, stirring until blended and smooth. Remove from heat; cool 5 minutes. Stir in the lime zest, ginger, oats, and coconut.

◆ Working quickly, drop by rounded teaspoonfuls onto wax-paper-lined sheets. Loosely cover with plastic wrap and refrigerate 2–3 hours. Let stand at room temperature about 15 minutes before serving. Store tightly covered in refrigerator. ◆ Makes about 36 cookies.

Drop Cookies

Cashew Butterscotchies

These four-ingredient treats are certain to liven up your lunch bag and become part of your favorite-cookie repertoire.

2	**cups butterscotch baking chips**
1	**teaspoon vanilla extract**
1$^1/_2$	**cups quick-cooking oats, uncooked**
1	**cup chopped, lightly salted, roasted cashews**

◇ Line cookie sheets with wax paper.

◇ Place butterscotch chips in a medium microwave-safe bowl. Microwave on high for 30–90 seconds or until mixture is melted and smooth, stirring every 30 seconds. Stir in vanilla, oats, and cashews; mix until well blended.

◇ Working quickly, drop by heaping teaspoonfuls onto wax-paper-lined sheets. Chill until firm. Store tightly covered in refrigerator. ◇ Makes about 36 cookies.

Drop Cookies

Chocolate-Covered Raisin Cookies

As good as these cookies are, you can also vary the flavor by using other types of chocolate or baking chips (e.g., milk or white chocolate chips, butterscotch chips, cinnamon chips, peanut butter chips) and the dried fruit of your choice.

1	cup semisweet chocolate chips
5	tablespoons butter
16	large marshmallows
1	teaspoon vanilla extract
2	cups quick-cooking oats, uncooked
3/4	cup raisins

◆ Line cookie sheets with wax paper.

◆ In a large saucepan melt the chocolate chips with the butter and marshmallows over low heat, stirring until blended and smooth. Remove from heat; cool 5 minutes. Stir in vanilla, oats, and raisins.

◆ Working quickly, drop by rounded teaspoonfuls onto wax-paper-lined sheets. Cover and refrigerate 2–3 hours. Let stand at room temperature about 15 minutes before serving. Store tightly covered in refrigerator. ◆ Makes about 36 cookies.

Drop Cookies

German Chocolate Cookies

These milk chocolate, toffee, and coconut cookies have all of the great flavor of German chocolate cake in drop cookie form and just a few minutes of preparation. Serve them up and wait for the "oohs" and "ahhs."

1	cup milk chocolate chips
5	tablespoons butter
16	large marshmallows
1	teaspoon vanilla
2	cups quick-cooking oats, uncooked
1	cup sweetened flake coconut
$^1/_2$	cup toffee baking bits
$^1/_2$	cup chopped pecans

❖ Line cookie sheets with wax paper.

❖ In a large saucepan melt the chocolate chips with the butter and marshmallows over low heat, stirring until smooth. Remove from heat; cool slightly. Stir in vanilla, oats, coconut, toffee bits, and pecans.

❖ Working quickly, drop by rounded teaspoonfuls onto wax-paper-lined sheets. Cover and refrigerate 2–3 hours. Let stand at room temperature about 15 minutes before serving. Store tightly covered in refrigerator. ❖ Makes about 36 cookies.

Drop Cookies

Special K Chewies

These classic caramel–peanut butter chews are an all-time favorite at my graduate school alma mater, Indiana University, where they have been prepared and served on campus for more than a generation. The mixture hardens quickly, so be sure to prep the cookie sheets before you start cooking.

$^1/_2$	**cup sugar**
$^1/_2$	**cup corn syrup**
$^3/_4$	**cup creamy peanut butter**
1	**teaspoon vanilla extract**
4	**cups Kellogg's® Special K® cereal**

◆ Line cookie sheets with wax paper.

◆ In a medium-size saucepan, combine the sugar and corn syrup. Bring mixture to a boil, cooking and stirring constantly, until sugar is completely dissolved. Remove from heat. Stir in the peanut butter and vanilla until blended and smooth.

◆ Add the cereal to the peanut butter mixture, stirring until well coated. Working quickly, drop the mixture by heaping teaspoonfuls onto the wax paper. Let stand in cool place to harden. Store tightly covered between layers of wax paper. ◆ Makes about 24 cookies.

Drop Cookies
SPECIAL K CHEWIES

Gingerbread Chews

These chewy drops have the lovely flavor of old-fashioned gingerbread. Scented with ginger, cinnamon, and cloves, they're all about cozy.

$^1/_2$	cup packed dark brown sugar
$^1/_2$	cup dark corn syrup
$^3/_4$	cup creamy peanut butter
1	teaspoon vanilla extract
$1^1/_4$	teaspoons ground ginger
$^3/_4$	teaspoon ground cinnamon
$^1/_8$	teaspoon ground cloves
4	cups crisp rice cereal

◆ Line cookie sheets with wax paper.

◆ In medium-size saucepan combine the brown sugar and corn syrup. Bring mixture to a boil, cooking and stirring constantly, until sugar is completely dissolved. Remove from heat. Stir in the peanut butter, vanilla, ginger, cinnamon, and cloves until blended and smooth.

◆ Add the cereal to the peanut butter mixture, stirring until well coated. Working quickly, drop the mixture by heaping teaspoonfuls onto the wax paper. Let stand in cool place to harden. Store tightly covered between layers of wax paper. ◆ Makes about 24 cookies.

Drop Cookies

Almond Apricot Drops

These crisp cookies disappear quickly whenever I make them, and I make them often because they are so simple to prepare and the recipe can easily be doubled for large gatherings, pitch-ins, or cookie trays.

2	cups Corn Chex® cereal, coarsely crushed
$^{1}/_{2}$	cup slivered almonds
$^{1}/_{2}$	cup chopped, dried apricots
1$^{1}/_{4}$	cups white chocolate chips
$^{1}/_{4}$	teaspoon almond extract

◇ Line cookie sheets with wax paper.

◇ In a large bowl combine the cereal, almonds, and apricots. Set aside momentarily.

◇ In a microwave-safe medium mixing bowl, melt the white chocolate chips on high for 2 minutes, stirring after 1 minute. Stir in the almond extract and then stir mixture into cereal mixture.

◇ Working quickly, drop by tablespoonfuls onto wax-paper-lined sheets. Let cool until firm. Store in airtight container between sheets of wax paper. ◇ Makes about 30 cookies.

Drop Cookies

Honey-Peanut Butter Puffs

Sweet and wholesome, these are Mom and kid favorites. They are a delicious and healthful alternative to candy and a frugal substitute for purchased energy bars.

$1/2$	cup firmly packed brown sugar
$1/4$	cup honey
1	tablespoon butter
$1/2$	cup creamy peanut butter
2	cups sweetened puffed wheat cereal

◆ Line cookie sheets with wax paper.

◆ In a medium-size saucepan combine the brown sugar and honey. Cook over medium heat, stirring frequently, until sugar is dissolved and mixture begins to bubble, about 4 minutes. Remove from heat.

◆ Blend in butter and peanut butter, stirring until melted and smooth. Add the cereal, stirring only until cereal is well coated. Working quickly, drop mixture by teaspoonfuls onto wax-paper-lined sheets. Let stand in cool place to harden. Store in airtight container between sheets of wax paper. ◆ Makes about 24 cookies.

Drop Cookies

Baby Ruthy Clusters

For a backyard barbecue or a fun-in-the-sun picnic, these cookie clusters have all the right ingredients (which can also be found in a favorite candy bar of similar name): milk chocolate, salty peanuts, and a hearty dose of gooey caramel to hold everything together.

12	caramels, unwrapped
$^1/_2$	cup milk chocolate chips
2	tablespoons milk
2	cups honey graham cereal, slightly crushed (yields about $1^1/_2$ cups crushed cereal)
$^3/_4$	cup very coarsely chopped lightly salted, roasted peanuts

❖ Line cookie sheets with wax paper. Lightly spray with nonstick cooking spray. Set aside momentarily.

❖ In a heavy medium saucepan combine the caramels, milk chocolate chips, and milk. Stir over low heat until caramels are melted. Remove from heat. Stir in cereal and peanuts.

❖ Working quickly, drop mixture from a teaspoon onto wax-paper-lined sheets. Let stand until firm. Store cookies in refrigerator up to 1 week. ❖ Makes about 28 cookies.

Drop Cookies

Rocky Road Drops

If you like marshmallows, chocolate chips, and peanuts, you'll love this cookie version of rocky road.

2	**cups sugar**
$^1/_2$	**cup (1 stick) butter**
$^1/_2$	**cup milk**
$^1/_3$	**cup unsweetened cocoa powder**
3	**cups quick-cooking oats, uncooked**
$^1/_3$	**cup chopped roasted, salted peanuts**
$^1/_3$	**cup semisweet chocolate chips**
2	**cups miniature marshmallows**

❖ Line cookie sheets with wax paper.

❖ In a large saucepan combine sugar, butter, milk, and cocoa. Bring to a boil over medium heat, stirring frequently. Continue boiling 3 minutes. Remove from heat.

❖ Stir in the oats, peanuts, chocolate chips, and marshmallows; mix well.

❖ Working quickly, drop by tablespoonfuls onto wax-paper-lined sheets. Let stand until set. Store tightly covered at room temperature. ❖ Makes about 48 cookies.

Drop Cookies
ROCKY ROAD DROPS

Peanut Butter Cookies

Peanut butter was one of the original health foods, invented in 1890 by a St. Louis doctor for an ailing patient and promoted in 1904 at the St. Louis Universal Exposition. It's been a favorite American food ever since. Celebrate its goodness with this delicious, no-bake take on peanut butter cookies.

$^1/_2$	**cup (1 stick) butter**
2	**cups packed dark brown sugar**
$^1/_2$	**cup canned evaporated milk**
$^1/_2$	**cup creamy peanut butter**
1	**teaspoon vanilla extract**
3	**cups quick-cooking oats, uncooked**
1	**cup roasted peanuts (optional)**

◆ Line cookie sheets with wax paper.

◆ In a large heavy saucepan combine the butter, brown sugar, and evaporated milk. Bring mixture to a boil over medium heat, stirring occasionally, until mixture comes to a full boil.

◆ Without stirring, let mixture boil for exactly 3 minutes. Immediately remove from heat. Stir in peanut butter and vanilla, stirring until peanut butter has melted. Quickly stir in the oats and, if desired, peanuts; mix well.

◆ Working quickly, drop mixture by kitchen tablespoonfuls onto wax-paper-lined sheets. Allow to cool and become firm, about 30 minutes. Store in covered container between sheets of wax paper in a cool, dry place. ◆ Makes about 36 cookies.

Drop Cookies

Bananas Foster Clusters

You can make these yummy treats without the alcohol by replacing the rum or brandy with 1½ tablespoons water combined with 1½ teaspoons rum-flavored or brandy-flavored baking extract.

12	caramels, unwrapped
½	cup white, milk, or semisweet chocolate chips
2	tablespoons dark rum or brandy
2	cups honey graham cereal, slightly crushed (about 1½ cups)
¾	cup coarsely crushed banana chips

◆ Line cookie sheets with wax paper.

◆ In a heavy medium saucepan combine the caramels, chocolate chips, and rum. Cook and stir over low heat until caramels are melted and mixture is smooth. Remove from heat. Stir in cereal and banana chips until blended.

◆ Working quickly, drop mixture from a kitchen teaspoon onto wax-paper-lined sheets. Let stand until firm (about 30 minutes). Store in covered container between sheets of wax paper. ◆ Makes about 28 clusters.

Drop Cookies

Haystacks

The crunch of crisp chow mein noodles and the smooth, rich taste of chocolate makes these long-standing favorites worth making time and time again.

1	3-ounce can chow mein noodles or 2 cups pretzel sticks, broken into $1/2$-inch pieces
1	cup dry-roasted peanuts
2	cups semisweet chocolate chips
1	14-ounce can sweetened condensed milk

◆ Line cookie sheets with wax paper.

◆ In a large bowl combine the noodles and peanuts; set aside.

◆ In a heavy medium saucepan set over low heat, melt the chocolate chips with the condensed milk, stirring until melted and smooth. Remove from heat.

◆ Stir warm chocolate mixture into noodle-peanut mixture. Working quickly, drop by tablespoonfuls onto prepared baking sheet; chill 2 hours or until firm. Store in covered container between sheets of wax paper. ◆ Makes about 36 cookies.

Variations:
Milk Chocolate Cashew Haystacks: Prepare as directed above but use milk chocolate chips in place of the semisweet chocolate chips and coarsely chopped roasted cashews in place of the peanuts.

White Chocolate Almond Haystacks: Prepare as directed above but use white chocolate chips in place of the semisweet chocolate chips. Add $1/2$ teaspoon almond extract to the melted chocolate mixture and use coarsely chopped roasted almonds in place of the peanuts.

Drop Cookies

Holiday Haystacks: Prepare as directed above but use white chocolate chips in place of the semisweet chocolate chips and a combination of $^1/_2$ cup dried cranberries plus $^1/_2$ cup coarsely chopped roasted almonds in place of the peanuts.

Butterscotch Haystacks: Prepare as directed above but use butterscotch baking chips in place of the semisweet chocolate chips.

Drop Cookies
HAYSTACKS

Oatmeal Raisin Cookies

On a cold winter evening, cozy up with one of these cookies in one hand and a steaming mug of cocoa in the other.

1	cup butterscotch baking chips
5	tablespoons butter
16	large marshmallows
$^1/_2$	teaspoon ground cinnamon
2	cups quick-cooking oats, uncooked
1	cup raisins
$^1/_2$	cup sweetened flake coconut

◇ Line cookie sheets with wax paper.

◇ In a large saucepan set over low heat, melt the butterscotch chips with the butter, marshmallows, and cinnamon, stirring until blended and smooth. Remove from heat; cool 5 minutes. Stir in oats, raisins, and coconut.

◇ Working quickly, drop by rounded teaspoonfuls onto wax-paper-lined sheets. Loosely cover with plastic wrap and refrigerate 2–3 hours. Let stand at room temperature about 15 minutes before serving. Store tightly covered in refrigerator. ◇ Makes about 36 cookies.

Drop Cookies

Fresh Apple Cookies

Apples just seem made for brown sugar and butter. With a combination this good, you won't need much else, save for time to enjoy.

$^1/_2$	cup (1 stick) butter
2	cups packed brown sugar
2	tablespoons flour
1	cup peeled, grated tart apple (e.g., Granny Smith)
$^1/_2$	teaspoon ground cinnamon
3	cups quick-cooking oats, uncooked
$^2/_3$	cup chopped walnuts or pecans
1	teaspoon vanilla extract

◆ Line cookie sheets with wax paper.

◆ In a medium saucepan melt the butter over medium heat. Add the brown sugar, flour, grated apple, and cinnamon. Bring mixture to a boil; boil 1 minute. Remove from heat and immediately add the oats, nuts, and vanilla, mixing until well blended.

◆ Working quickly, drop by heaping teaspoonfuls onto wax-paper-lined sheets. Loosely cover with plastic wrap and refrigerate at least 1 hour until firm. Store tightly covered in refrigerator. ◆ Makes about 40 cookies.

Variation:
Fresh Pear & Nutmeg Cookies: Prepare as directed above but substitute 1 cup grated fresh pear for the apple and $^1/_4$ teaspoon ground nutmeg for the cinnamon.

Drop Cookies
FRESH APPLE COOKIES

Dark Chocolate Hazelnut Cookies

The confectionary combination of hazelnuts and chocolate is very popular throughout Europe, particularly Italy, where it is known as gianduia. Deep and rich in chocolate flavor, these cookies are sure to top your list of chocolate favorites.

$^1/_2$	cup (1 stick) butter
2	1-ounce squares unsweetened baking chocolate, chopped
$1^3/_4$	cups sugar
$^1/_3$	cup milk
$^1/_2$	cup chocolate hazelnut spread (e.g., Nutella)
1	teaspoon vanilla extract
3	cups quick-cooking oats, uncooked

◆ Line cookie sheets with wax paper.

◆ In a large heavy saucepan melt the butter and unsweetened chocolate over medium heat, stirring constantly until melted and smooth. Add the sugar and milk; continue stirring until mixture comes to a full rolling boil. Let mixture boil for exactly 3 minutes without stirring. Immediately remove the pan from heat.

◆ Stir in the hazelnut spread and vanilla, stirring until the hazelnut spread has melted. Quickly stir in the oats, mixing well.

◆ Working quickly, drop the mixture by tablespoonfuls onto wax-paper-lined sheets. Allow to cool about 30 minutes until cookies are firm. Store tightly covered between sheets of wax paper. ◆ Makes about 24 cookies.

Drop Cookies

Coffee Toffee Cookies

This is a rich, comforting cookie, reminiscent of favorite flavored espresso drinks from the local coffee shop. Tuck one of these in your lunch bag or briefcase for a late-afternoon pick-me-up.

2	cups packed dark brown sugar
$^3/_4$	cup (1$^1/_2$ sticks) butter
1	5-ounce can ($^2/_3$ cup) evaporated milk
1	4-serving-size package instant butterscotch pudding mix
2$^1/_4$	teaspoons instant coffee or espresso powder
2$^1/_2$	cups quick-cooking oats, uncooked

◆ Line cookie sheets with wax paper.

◆ In a large heavy saucepan combine the brown sugar, butter, and evaporated milk. Cook and stir until mixture comes to a full rolling boil. Remove the pan from heat.

◆ Stir in the pudding mix, coffee powder, and oats, mixing well.

◆ Working quickly, drop the mixture by tablespoonfuls onto wax-paper-lined sheets. Allow to cool and become firm, about 30 minutes. ◆ Makes about 24 cookies.

Drop Cookies

Triple Chocolate Chippers

Chocolate times three equals cookie perfection in these fast and fudge-y cookies.

1¹/₂	**cups sugar**
¹/₂	**cup (1 stick) butter**
1	**5-ounce can (²/₃ cup) evaporated milk**
1¹/₃	**cups miniature semisweet chocolate chips, divided use**
1	**4-serving-size package instant chocolate pudding mix**
1	**teaspoon vanilla extract**
2¹/₂	**cups quick-cooking oats, uncooked**

◆ Line cookie sheets with wax paper.

◆ In a large heavy saucepan combine the sugar, butter, and evaporated milk. Cook and stir until mixture comes to a full rolling boil. Remove the pan from heat and stir in ¹/₃ cup of the chocolate chips until melted and smooth.

◆ Stir in the pudding mix, vanilla, and oats, mixing well. Stir in the remaining 1 cup chocolate chips.

◆ Working quickly, drop the mixture by tablespoonfuls onto wax-paper-lined sheets. Allow to cool about 30 minutes until firm. ◆ Makes about 24 cookies.

Drop Cookies

Salty-Sweet Chocolate Crispy Chews

If you have a penchant for the combination of salty and sweet, this is your cookie.

2	cups semisweet, milk, or white chocolate chips or butter-scotch baking chips
1/2	cup chunky peanut butter
1	teaspoon vanilla extract
1 1/2	cups miniature marshmallows
1	cup lightly salted mixed nuts, coarsely chopped
1	cup crisp rice cereal

◆ Line cookie sheets with wax paper.

◆ In a microwave-safe medium mixing bowl melt the chips on high for 2 minutes, stirring after every 30 seconds. Stir in the peanut butter and vanilla until blended. Stir in the marshmallows, nuts, and cereal.

◆ Working quickly, drop by small spoonfuls onto prepared wax-paper-lined sheets. Store in a covered container in a cool place. ◆ Makes about 24 cookies.

Drop Cookies

Orange Cream Clusters

Ramen noodles may sound like an unusual ingredient for cookies, but you'll be convinced after your first nibble. They add a delicate crispiness that deliciously complements the citrus-cream flavor of these teatime treats.

3	packages (3 ounces each) ramen noodles (any flavor)
$^1/_2$	cup sliced almonds
$^1/_4$	cup ($^1/_2$ stick) butter
1	tablespoon grated orange zest
1	cup white chocolate chips

◆ Line cookie sheets with wax paper.

◆ Place the uncooked noodles in a large bowl. Discard noodle seasoning packets or save for another use. Break up noodles into small pieces ($^1/_2$ inch or smaller) with fingers or a wooden spoon. Add almonds to the bowl.

◆ In a large skillet set over medium heat melt the butter. Add the noodle mixture. Cook over medium heat, stirring constantly, for about 5 minutes or until noodles and almonds just begin to brown. Transfer mixture from skillet back to large bowl; add the orange zest, stirring to combine. Cool slightly.

◆ In a medium, uncovered, microwave-safe bowl melt the white chocolate chips on medium-high (70 percent power) for 1 minute; stir. Microwave at additional 10- to 15-second intervals, stirring just until chocolate is melted. Pour melted chocolate over noodle mixture in bowl. Toss until noodle mixture is completely coated.

◆ Working quickly, drop by rounded teaspoonfuls into mounds onto prepared wax-paper-lined sheets (mixture will appear loose, but will set as it cools). Let stand for 45–60 minutes or until set. Store in covered container between sheets of wax paper. ◆ Makes 24 cookies.

Drop Cookies

Variations:

Lime Cream Cookies: Prepare as directed above but substitute lime zest for the orange zest.

Butter Pecan Cookie Clusters: Prepare as directed above but omit the orange zest. Use chopped pecans in place of the almonds and add $^3/_4$ teaspoon vanilla extract to the melted white chocolate before adding the ramen noodle mixture.

Drop Cookies

Coconut Cashew Cookies

Cashews are as tropical as coconut, originating in South America but also widely cultivated in many tropical countries. The two flavors pair deliciously in these easy drops that require no cooking at all.

1	cup cashew butter or creamy peanut butter
1	cup powdered sugar
$^1/_2$	cup milk
1	teaspoon vanilla extract
2	cups uncooked oats (quick or old-fashioned)
1	cup coarsely chopped, lightly salted roasted cashews
1	cup sweetened flake coconut

◇ Line cookie sheets with wax paper.

◇ In a large bowl combine the cashew butter, powdered sugar, milk, and vanilla with a wooden spoon until well blended. Stir in oats, cashews, and coconut until mixture is well blended.

◇ Drop by kitchen teaspoonfuls onto prepared wax-paper-lined sheets. Store tightly covered in a cool, dry place. ◇ Makes about 48 cookies.

Drop Cookies

Maple Cranberry Cookies

The aromatic flavor of maple makes for a particularly fine fall cookie, especially when punctuated with tart-sweet bits of dried cranberries.

2	cups white chocolate chips
$^1/_4$	cup creamy peanut butter
2	teaspoons maple-flavored extract
3	cups crisp rice cereal
1	cup dried cranberries

◆ Line cookie sheets with wax paper.

◆ Place the white chocolate chips and peanut butter in a large, uncovered, microwavable bowl.

◆ Microwave on medium-high (70 percent power) for 1 minute; stir. If necessary, microwave at additional 10- to 15-second intervals, stirring just until chips are melted. Stir in the maple extract. Stir in the cereal and cranberries until combined.

◆ Working quickly, drop by rounded tablespoonfuls onto prepared wax-paper-lined sheets; let stand until set. Store tightly covered in a cool, dry place. ◆ Makes 36 cookies.

Drop Cookies

S'mores Clusters

Kids of all ages will appreciate the decadent campfire combination of chocolate, marshmallows, and graham crackers in these easily assembled cookie clusters.

2	**cups semisweet chocolate chips**
3	**cups miniature marshmallows**
12	**whole honey graham crackers, broken into bite-sized pieces**

◆ Line cookie sheets with wax paper.

◆ Place chocolate chips in large microwave-safe bowl. Microwave on high for 2 minutes, stopping every 30 seconds to stir chocolate, until chocolate is melted.

◆ Stir the marshmallows and graham pieces into the melted chocolate until evenly coated.

◆ Working quickly, drop tablespoonfuls of the s'more mixture onto wax-paper-lined cookie sheets. Refrigerate 30 minutes or until chocolate is set. Store in covered container in refrigerator. ◆ Makes about 36 clusters.

Drop Cookies

Ginger-Macadamia Tropi-Clusters

Anyone with a sweet tooth and a penchant for the peppery flavor of ginger will be delighted with these tropical-inspired cookies.

5	**cups cornflakes cereal**
1	**cup sweetened flake coconut**
$^1/_2$	**cup chopped, lightly salted macadamia nuts**
$^1/_2$	**cup (1 stick) butter**
$4^1/_2$	**cups miniature marshmallows**
2	**teaspoons ground ginger**
$1^1/_2$	**teaspoons rum-flavored extract**

◆ Line cookie sheets with wax paper.

◆ In a large bowl mix the cornflakes, coconut, and macadamia nuts.

◆ In large saucepan set over low heat melt the butter. Add marshmallows; stir until marshmallows are melted and mixture is smooth. Remove from heat and stir in ginger and rum extract. Pour over cornflakes mixture; toss until well coated.

◆ Working quickly, drop by tablespoonfuls onto prepared wax-paper-lined sheets. Cool completely. Store in covered container between sheets of wax paper. ◆ Makes about 40 cookies.

Drop Cookies

Lemon-Honey Clusters

Ready for a new taste treat? Try these lemony, crispy clusters, scented with coriander, citrus zest, and honey.

$5^1/_4$	cups honey-nut cornflakes cereal
$^1/_2$	cup sliced almonds
$^1/_2$	cup (1 stick) butter
$3^3/_4$	cups miniature marshmallows
$^1/_3$	cup honey
1	tablespoon grated lemon zest
$^1/_2$	teaspoon ground coriander (optional)

◆ Line cookie sheets with wax paper.

◆ Mix the cornflakes and almonds in a large bowl.

◆ In a large saucepan on low heat melt the butter. Add the marshmallows and honey; cook and stir until marshmallows are completely melted and mixture is smooth. Remove from heat and stir in the lemon zest and ground coriander, if desired, until blended.

◆ Pour marshmallow mixture over corn flake mixture, tossing to coat well.

◆ Working quickly, drop by rounded tablespoonfuls onto prepared wax-paper-lined sheets. Cool completely. Store, tightly covered, in a cool, dry place. ◆ Makes about 40 clusters.

Drop Cookies

Mocha Puffs

Chocolate and coffee team up for a simple, and simply delicious, little cookie.

4	1-ounce squares semisweet baking chocolate, chopped
2	tablespoons chocolate hazelnut spread (e.g., Nutella)
1	teaspoon instant espresso or coffee powder
2¹/₂	cups sweetened puffed wheat cereal

◆ Line cookie sheets with wax paper.

◆ In a large microwavable bowl microwave the chocolate, hazelnut spread, and espresso powder on high for 1¹/₂–2 minutes or until chocolate is almost melted, stopping and stirring every 30 seconds. Stir until chocolate is completely melted. Stir in cereal.

◆ Working quickly, drop by teaspoonfuls onto prepared wax-paper-lined sheets.

◆ Refrigerate until firm. Store in tightly covered container in refrigerator.
◆ Makes about 30 cookies.

Drop Cookies
MOCHA PUFFS

Shaped Cookies

Snickery Crispy Cookie Balls

Tempt the candy lovers you know with these crispy, candy bar treats. The cookies can also be made in bar form. Simply press the mixture into a 13x9x2-inch baking pan that has been lightly sprayed with cooking spray, then cut into bars when cool.

¹/₂	cup (1 stick) butter
1	10-ounce bag miniature marshmallows
2	2.15-ounce chocolate-covered caramel and nougat candy bars, chopped (e.g., Snickers®)
6	cups crisp rice cereal
	Decorator sugars, decorator candies, sprinkles, or miniature semisweet chocolate chips (optional)

◆ Melt butter over medium-low heat in 4-quart saucepan. Stir in marshmallows until melted. Remove from heat; stir in candy bars and cereal until blended.

◆ Shape mixture into 1-inch balls with buttered hands. If desired, roll the balls in decorator sugars, decorator candies, sprinkles, or miniature chocolate chips. Place on wax paper. Store in airtight containers between sheets of wax paper. ◆ Makes about 48 small cookie balls.

Shaped Cookies

Almond Coffee Cookie Balls

For an extra-special presentation, consider drizzling some melted white or dark chocolate over each cookie ball. Refrigerate 30 minutes until set and then serve.

2	cups finely crushed plain sugar cookies (about 8 ounces)
1	cup sliced almonds, finely chopped
$^1/_4$	cup light corn syrup
2	tablespoons coffee-flavored liqueur
$^1/_2$	teaspoon almond extract
2	tablespoons butter, melted
$1^2/_3$	cups sifted powdered sugar, divided use

◆ In a large mixing bowl combine the crushed cookies, chopped almonds, corn syrup, coffee liqueur, almond extract, butter, and 1 cup of the powdered sugar with a wooden spoon until well blended. Shape mixture into 1-inch balls.

◆ Place remaining $^2/_3$ cup powdered sugar in shallow dish or bowl. Roll balls in powdered sugar; loosely cover with plastic wrap. Let stand 2 hours. If desired, roll again in additional powdered sugar. Chill up to 1 week or freeze up to 3 months. ◆ Makes about 40 cookie balls.

Shaped Cookies

Cranberry Cereal Wreaths

Delight everyone on your gift list with these irresistible treats. They're the perfect way to show how much you care.

4$^1/_2$	**cups cornflakes**
1	**cup miniature marshmallows**
$^1/_3$	**cup chopped almonds**
$^2/_3$	**cup dried cranberries**
3	**cups vanilla baking chips or white chocolate chips**
$^3/_4$	**teaspoon almond extract**
	Purchased small tubes of green and/or red decorating icing (optional)

❖ Line cookie sheets with wax paper.

❖ In a large mixing bowl combine the cornflakes, marshmallows, almonds, and dried cranberries.

❖ In a heavy medium saucepan melt the vanilla chips over very low heat, stirring until completely melted and smooth; stir in almond extract. Pour mixture over cereal mixture; stir gently until well coated.

❖ Drop mixture by $^1/_4$-cupfuls onto the prepared cookie sheets. Flatten mixture slightly to form circles about 2 inches wide. Using the handle of a wooden spoon, make a $^3/_4$-inch hole in the center of each cookie to form a wreath shape, spreading the cookies to about 3 inches in diameter.

❖ When cool, decorate with frosting, if desired. Place wreaths in an airtight container with wax paper between layers. Seal and store at room temperature up to 3 days. ❖ Makes about 15 cookie wreaths.

Shaped Cookies

Valentine's Day Chocolate-Mint Hearts

You're sure to win a few hearts with these pretty and very delicious crispy cookies.

1	cup semisweet chocolate chips
1/4	cup light corn syrup
2	tablespoons butter
1/2	teaspoon peppermint extract
3	cups crisp rice cereal
	Purchased small tubes of pink and/or red decorating icing (optional)

◆ Line cookie sheets with wax paper.

◆ In a heavy medium saucepan set over low heat melt the chocolate chips with the corn syrup and butter, stirring with a wooden spoon until melted and smooth. Remove from heat and stir in peppermint extract. Gently stir in rice cereal with a wooden spoon until the cereal is evenly coated with chocolate.

◆ Immediately turn the chocolate-coated cereal out onto the wax-paper-lined cookie sheet. Pat mixture into a 12x6-inch rectangle. Chill about 20 minutes or until slightly firm.

◆ Cut cereal mixture into heart shapes with a 3-inch heart-shaped cookie cutter. Decorate with frosting, if desired. Chill until firm; wrap each heart in plastic wrap. Store cookies in refrigerator up to 1 week. ◆ Makes 8 or 9 cookies.

Shaped Cookies

Orange & Cardamom Cookie Balls

Looking for a different kind of cookie? Try whipping up a batch of these elegant little cookies perfumed with cardamom and citrus.

2	cups finely crushed plain sugar cookies (about 8 ounces)
1	cup sliced almonds, finely chopped
$^1/_4$	cup light corn syrup
2	tablespoons thawed orange juice concentrate (undiluted)
2	teaspoons grated orange zest
$^1/_2$	teaspoon ground cardamom
2	tablespoons butter, melted
1 $^2/_3$	cup sifted powdered sugar, divided use

❖ In a large mixing bowl combine the crushed cookies, chopped almonds, corn syrup, orange juice concentrate, orange zest, cardamom, melted butter, and 1 cup of the powdered sugar with a wooden spoon until well blended. Shape mixture into 1-inch balls.

❖ Place remaining $^2/_3$ cup powdered sugar in shallow dish or bowl. Roll balls in powdered sugar; loosely cover with plastic wrap. Let stand 2 hours. If desired, roll again in additional powdered sugar. Chill up to 1 week or freeze up to 3 months. ❖ Makes about 40 cookie balls.

Spiced Pecan Bourbon Balls

Looking for a special-occasion cookie? This is it. Coffee, cocoa, pecans, bourbon? Few things could make these any better, except perhaps the addition of a lazy summer afternoon.

2^1/$_2$	cups finely ground vanilla wafers
2	tablespoons unsweetened cocoa powder
1	cup finely chopped pecans
1	tablespoon instant espresso or coffee powder
^{1}/$_4$	teaspoon ground cinnamon
3	tablespoons light corn syrup
1^2/$_3$	cups powdered sugar, divided use
^{1}/$_3$	cup bourbon

◆ In a large bowl combine the vanilla wafer crumbs, cocoa powder, chopped pecans, espresso powder, cinnamon, corn syrup, and 1 cup powdered sugar, until combined. Stir in enough of the bourbon for mixture to hold together easily.

◆ Place remaining ^{2}/$_3$ cup powdered sugar in shallow dish or bowl. Roll balls in powdered sugar; cover. Let stand 2 hours. If desired, roll again in additional powdered sugar. Chill up to 1 week or freeze up to 3 months in an airtight container between layers of wax paper. ◆ Makes about 36 cookie balls.

Shaped Cookies

SPICED PECAN BOURBON BALLS

Date Dainties

Dates are so sweet and flavorful, why relegate them to granola and holiday breads alone? The rich flavor here is far greater than the sum of this cookie's parts.

1	cup sweetened flake coconut
1	cup packed light brown sugar
1	cup finely chopped, pitted dates
2	large eggs, lightly beaten
1	teaspoon vanilla extract
3	cups crisp rice cereal

◆ Line cookie sheets with wax paper.

◆ Place the coconut into a shallow dish or pie plate; set aside.

◆ In a cold, 12-inch frying pan, combine the brown sugar, dates, and eggs. Cook about 10 minutes over medium heat, stirring constantly, or until mixture starts to thicken and sugar is dissolved. Remove from heat.

◆ Stir the vanilla and cereal into the hot date mixture, mixing until well blended.

◆ Working quickly, dip a teaspoon in ice water, then drop rounded teaspoonfuls of mixture onto prepared sheets. Roll each cookie in coconut. Chill at least 1 hour before serving. Store in airtight container in refrigerator. ◆ Makes about 36 cookies.

Shaped Cookies

Caramel-Mallow Goodies

Part cookie, part candy, entirely delicious.

$^1/_2$	cup (1 stick) butter
1	14-ounce bag caramels, unwrapped
1	14-ounce can sweetened condensed milk
1	16-ounce bag regular marshmallows
5–7	cups crisp rice cereal

◇ Line cookie sheets with wax paper.

◇ In a medium saucepan set over low heat melt the butter and caramels, stirring constantly. Remove from heat. Whisk in the condensed milk until blended and smooth.

◇ Spread the cereal in $^1/_4$-inch layer in a lipped jelly roll pan. Using a fork, dip one marshmallow at a time in caramel mixture (coating thoroughly). Roll coated marshmallows in cereal until well coated. Place coated marshmallow on prepared sheets. Repeat with remaining marshmallows.

◇ Refrigerate coated marshmallows for 30 minutes before serving. Store in the refrigerator in an airtight container for up to 3–4 days. ◇ Makes about 36 cookies.

Shaped Cookies

Raspberry Pinwheels

This almond-laced, raspberry preserves-filled cookie takes the crispy rice cookie to delectable new heights.

$^1/_4$	cup ($^1/_2$ stick) butter
4	cups miniature marshmallows
$^1/_2$	teaspoon almond extract
6	cups crisp rice cereal
1	cup seedless raspberry preserves, room temperature

◆ Spray a 15x10x1-inch pan with nonstick cooking spray; set aside momentarily.

◆ In large saucepan melt the butter over low heat. Add the marshmallows and stir until completely melted. Cook over low heat 3 minutes longer, stirring constantly. Remove from heat and stir in almond extract. Add cereal and stir until well coated.

◆ Using a piece of wax paper, press mixture evenly into prepared pan. Cool completely.

◆ Stir preserves to loosen. Spread preserves over cereal mixture almost to edges. Cut in half crosswise. Roll up each half jelly-roll fashion, starting with cut edge. Wrap tightly in wax paper, sealing ends. Chill 1–2 hours or until firm. Cut into $^1/_2$-inch slices. Best if served the same day. ◆ Makes about 3 dozen slices.

Shaped Cookies

Apricot Petites

Lush, fragrant apricots show off their versatility in these quick-to-assemble cookies.

2	cups crushed vanilla wafers (about 40–45 wafers)
$^1/_2$	cup finely chopped dried apricots
$^1/_2$	cup finely chopped pecans or walnuts
$^1/_4$	teaspoon ground nutmeg
$1^2/_3$	cups powdered sugar, divided use
$^1/_4$	cup apricot nectar or orange juice
3	tablespoons light corn syrup
2	tablespoons ($^1/_4$ stick) butter, melted

❖ In a medium bowl combine vanilla wafers, dried apricots, pecans, nutmeg, and 1 cup of the powdered sugar; mix well. Add the apricot nectar, corn syrup, and melted butter; mix well with a wooden spoon.

❖ Place the remaining $^2/_3$ cup powdered sugar in a pie plate or other shallow dish. Shape mixture into 1-inch balls. Roll in powdered sugar. Cover tightly. Let stand 24 hours to blend flavors. Store in airtight container in refrigerator. ❖ Makes about 36 cookies.

Shaped Cookies
APRICOT PETITES

Butter Pecan Thumbprints

Some cookies transcend their short list of ingredients—you can't imagine how delicious they are until you taste the final product. These are such cookies.

1	16-ounce container prepared caramel-flavored frosting
$1/4$	cup ($1/2$ stick) butter, softened
$2^1/2$	cups graham cracker crumbs
1	teaspoon butter pecan extract
1	cup very finely ground pecans
48	white chocolate-striped "Hugs" kisses, unwrapped

◆ Line a cookie sheet with wax paper.

◆ In a large bowl beat the frosting and butter with an electric mixer set on medium speed until well blended and smooth. Mix in graham cracker crumbs and butter pecan extract with a wooden spoon until combined.

◆ Place ground pecans in a pie pan or shallow dish. Shape graham cracker mixture into 1-inch balls. Roll each ball in pecans to coat. Place balls on prepared sheets.

◆ Press one chocolate candy into the center of each cookie. Refrigerate for 30 minutes or until cold. Store leftovers tightly covered in refrigerator for up to 1 week. ◆ Makes 48 cookies.

Variation:
Double Chocolate Kiss Cookies: Prepare as directed above but use chocolate frosting in place of caramel frosting, vanilla extract in place of butter pecan extract, and milk chocolate kisses in place of "hugs."

Strawberry Cheesecake Thumbprints

The tanginess of cream cheese partners deliciously with strawberry jam in these rich and pretty cookies.

1	16-ounce container prepared cream cheese frosting
4	ounces ($^1/_2$ of an 8-ounce package) cream cheese, softened
$2^1/_2$	cups crisp sugar cookie or crisp macaroon crumbs
$^1/_2$	teaspoon almond extract
1	cup very finely ground almonds
$^1/_2$	cup strawberry jam, room temperature

◇ Line a cookie sheet with wax paper.

◇ In a large bowl beat the frosting and cream cheese with an electric mixer set to medium speed until well blended and smooth. Mix in cookie crumbs and almond extract with a wooden spoon until combined.

◇ Place ground almonds in a pie pan or shallow dish. Shape cookie mixture into 1-inch balls. Roll each ball in almonds to coat. Place balls on cookie sheet. Make an indentation with thumb or back of a $^1/_4$-teaspoon measure into the center of each cookie.

◇ Fill each indentation with $^1/_4$ teaspoon jam. Refrigerate for 30 minutes or until cold. Store leftovers tightly covered in refrigerator for up to 1 week. ◇ Makes about 45 cookies.

Shaped Cookies

Caramel Delightfuls

Perfect lunch-box or after-school treats, these caramel-coconut cookies will be surefire hits with one and all.

2¹/₂	**dozen square shortbread cookies (e.g., Lorna Doones®)**
6	**tablespoons (³/₄ stick) butter**
¹/₂	**cup packed dark brown sugar**
¹/₂	**cup light corn syrup**
¹/₂	**cup sweetened condensed milk**
¹/₂	**teaspoon vanilla extract**
4	**cups sweetened flake coconut, skillet toasted (see page 8) and cooled**
1	**cup semisweet chocolate chips**

◆ Place each shortbread cookie on cookie sheets lined with wax paper.

◆ In medium saucepan set over medium-low heat combine the butter, brown sugar, and corn syrup. Bring mixture to a full boil, stirring constantly with a wooden spoon. Boil 3 minutes, stirring constantly.

◆ Slowly pour in sweetened condensed milk, stirring constantly. Continue cooking over low heat 5 minutes, stirring constantly. Remove the pan from the heat; stir in the vanilla. Beat with an electric mixer set on medium-high speed 3–4 minutes until creamy.

◆ Immediately stir in toasted coconut and mix well. Spoon mixture by teaspoonfuls over shortbread cookies. Cool completely.

◆ Melt chocolate chips in small microwavable bowl in microwave for 1–2 minutes; drizzle thinly in stripes over cookies and let chocolate harden at room temperature. Store in airtight container. ◆ Makes about 30 cookies.

Shaped Cookies
CARAMEL DELIGHTFULS

Slim Mint Chocolate Wafers

Smooth and cool, these chocolate-mint wafers—a variation on a favorite girl troop cookie—are always winners, even with people who claim they do not like mint.

1	**12-ounce bag (2 cups) semisweet chocolate chips**
1	**tablespoon vegetable shortening**
1	**teaspoon peppermint extract**
36	**round buttery crackers (e.g., Ritz)**

◆ Line two cookie sheets with wax paper.

◆ In a large heavy saucepan melt the chocolate chips and shortening over low heat, stirring until melted and smooth; stir in peppermint extract until blended.

◆ Working quickly, drop crackers, one at a time, into melted chocolate, coating completely. Remove with 2 forks and place on prepared cookie sheets. Repeat with remaining crackers and chocolate (if chocolate mixture becomes too thick, rewarm for 1–2 minutes over low heat, stirring until melted).

◆ Refrigerate for 20 minutes or until set. Store leftovers, tightly covered, in refrigerator for up to 1 week. ◆ Makes 36 cookies.

Shaped Cookies

Chocolate Whiskey Balls

If you think this is just another cookie, think again—you may be surprised by the magic wrought by combining chocolate and whiskey.

1	**cup pecans**
1	**cup chocolate wafer cookie crumbs**
1^1/$_2$	**tablespoons light corn syrup**
^{1}/$_4$	**cup whiskey**
1^1/$_2$	**cups powdered sugar, divided use**

❖ Grind the pecans and the chocolate wafers coarsely in a large food processor. Transfer mixture to a large bowl. Mix in corn syrup, whiskey, and 1 cup of the powdered sugar with wooden spoon or hands until well blended.

❖ Place remaining ^{1}/$_2$ cup powdered sugar in shallow dish or bowl. Roll balls in powdered sugar; cover. Let stand 2 hours. If desired, roll again in additional powdered sugar. Chill up to 1 week or freeze up to 3 months. ❖ Makes about 24 cookie balls.

Variation:
Chocolate Grand Marnier Balls: Prepare as directed above but use Grand Marnier or other orange liqueur in place of the whiskey and add 2 teaspoons grated orange zest to the mixture along with the cookie crumbs.

Shaped Cookies

Reindeer Pretzel Treats

At holiday time, everyone needs a few cookie recipes that are extra good and extra easy. That way, a gift-worthy cookie plate for a friend, neighbor, teacher, or colleague can be assembled in short order. These adorable reindeer cookies fit the bill—they're as cute as they are delicious.

36	large pretzel twists
$^1/_2$	cup (1 stick) butter
1	10-ounce bag miniature marshmallows
3	tablespoons unsweetened cocoa powder
5	cups chocolate or plain crisp rice cereal
36	red cinnamon candies
72	mini chocolate chips or candies

◆ Line two cookie sheets with wax paper.

◆ Carefully break off the very top of the two curved loops on each pretzel so that each pretzel resembles a pair of antlers; set aside.

◆ In a large saucepan or Dutch oven set over low heat melt the butter and marshmallows with the cocoa powder, stirring constantly, until marshmallows are melted and mixture is well blended. Add cereal; gently stir until well coated.

◆ Drop cereal mixture by buttered tablespoonfuls onto prepared sheets (36 mounds total). Using buttered hands, shape each mound into an oval shape (to resemble a reindeer head). Quickly push 1 pretzel piece into top of each oval to resemble the antlers. Press in cinnamon candy for red nose and chocolate chips for eyes. Cool completely. Store between sheets of wax paper in airtight container. ◆ Makes 36 cookies.

Shaped Cookies
REINDEER PRETZEL TREATS

Rum Raisin Cookie Balls

Oh-so-delicious, these grown-up cookies are guaranteed favorites thanks to a hearty dose of dark rum.

$^1/_2$	cup quick-cooking oats
$^1/_3$	cup dark rum
2	cups powdered sugar
$^2/_3$	cup sweetened flake coconut
$^2/_3$	cup ground pecans
$^2/_3$	cup golden raisins
3	tablespoons unsweetened cocoa
$^1/_4$	teaspoon ground nutmeg
6	tablespoons ($^3/_4$ stick) butter, melted
$^1/_3$	cup sugar

❖ In a large bowl combine the oats and rum. Cover; let stand 1 hour.

❖ Add the powdered sugar, coconut, pecans, raisins, cocoa, nutmeg, and butter to the rum-oats mixture; mix well with a wooden spoon or hands. Cover with plastic wrap and refrigerate until firm, at least 2 hours.

❖ Place the sugar in a shallow dish. Roll heaping teaspoonfuls of cookie mixture into 1-inch balls. Roll in sugar to coat evenly. Store at least 2 days in airtight container at room temperature to blend flavors. ❖ Makes about 48 cookie balls.

Shaped Cookies

Peanut Butter Honey Bees

Involve the entire family with this recipe. Even the youngest members of the family can help shape the bee bodies or stick in a few chow mein antennae.

1³/₄	cups creamy-style peanut butter
¹/₂	cup (1 stick) butter, softened
¹/₄	cup honey
1³/₄	cups powdered sugar
3	cups graham cracker crumbs
¹/₂	cup semi-sweet real chocolate chips
1	teaspoon vegetable shortening
¹/₃	cup sliced almonds
¹/₂	cup chow mein noodles

◆ Line two cookie sheets with wax paper.

◆ In a large bowl combine the peanut butter and butter. Beat with an electric mixer set on medium speed, scraping bowl often, until creamy, about 1–2 minutes.

◆ Add the honey and powdered sugar; reduce speed to low. Beat until well mixed, about 1–2 minutes. Stir in the graham cracker crumbs with a wooden spoon. Shape rounded tablespoonfuls of mixture into 1¹/₂-inch ovals. Place onto prepared cookie sheets.

◆ In small microwave-safe bowl combine the chocolate chips and shortening. Microwave on high for 30 seconds; stir. Continue microwaving at 10-second intervals, stirring until mixture is melted and smooth. Cool 2 minutes.

◆ Place chocolate in small plastic zip-top bag. Cut very small tip from one corner of bag.

Shaped Cookies

◆ For each honey bee, pipe 3 chocolate stripes crosswise on each oval; insert 2 almond slices in each side for wings. Insert 2 chow mein noodles in head for antenna; insert 1 short chow mein noodle for tail. Dot with chocolate for eyes, if desired. Refrigerate until firm, about 30 minutes. Store in refrigerator in a tightly covered container. ◆ Makes about 50 "bees."

Baker's Note: If dough is too soft, stir in additional powdered sugar, 1 tablespoon at a time, until desired consistency.

Tart Cherry-Date Skillet Cookies

Need lots of treats in a hurry for a party or potluck? Here's the solution. You don't need to like dates to love these cookies. The dates create a brown sugar-butter complement to the tart dried cherries, making for a cookie to be enjoyed by all.

1	cup (2 sticks) butter
1	cup firmly packed light or dark brown sugar
1	8-ounce package chopped dates
1	large egg, lightly beaten
3	cups crisp rice cereal
1	cup chopped tart dried cherries or dried cranberries
1	tablespoon vanilla extract
3½	cups sweetened flake coconut

◇ In a large skillet melt the butter; stir in the brown sugar and dates. Remove from heat. Stir in the egg; return to heat. Cook over medium heat, stirring constantly, until mixture comes to a full boil, about 4–6 minutes. Boil, stirring constantly, 1 minute.

◇ Remove from heat; stir in the cereal, dried cherries, vanilla, and 1 cup of the coconut until blended. Let stand 10 minutes.

◇ Place the remaining coconut in a shallow dish or pie plate. Shape rounded teaspoonfuls into 1-inch balls and roll in remaining coconut. ◇ Makes about 60 cookies.

Shaped Cookies

Cranberry-Almond Slices

These marshmallow and cranberry-flecked treats look like miniature mosaics.

1	cup butterscotch baking chips
2	tablespoons ($^1/_4$ stick) butter
1	14-ounce can sweetened condensed milk
$^3/_4$	teaspoon almond extract
3	cups graham cracker crumbs
2	cups miniature marshmallows
$^3/_4$	cup coarsely chopped honey-roasted almonds
$^3/_4$	cup chopped dried cranberries

◆ Set aside two 20-inch pieces of wax paper.

◆ In heavy saucepan set over low heat melt the butterscotch chips and butter with the condensed milk, stirring until blended and smooth. Stir in the almond extract.

◆ In a large bowl combine the graham cracker crumbs, marshmallows, almonds, and cranberries; stir in the butterscotch mixture. Divide mixture in half. Place each portion on a piece of the prepared wax paper; let stand 10 minutes.

◆ Using the wax paper as an aid, shape each portion into a 12-inch log. Wrap each log tightly; chill for 2 hours or until firm. Remove paper and cut each log into 15 slices. Store covered in refrigerator. ◆ Makes about 30 cookies.

Shaped Cookies

Caramel Toffee Tassies

Perfect for pitch-ins, these caramel-toffee-loaded treats both travel and keep well.

$^1/_4$	cup ($^1/_2$ stick) butter
1	10-ounce package miniature marshmallows
1	teaspoon vanilla extract
7	cups crisp rice cereal
4	chocolate-covered English toffee candy bars
1	cup caramel apple dip

◆ Lightly spray the cups of two 12-count muffin tins with nonstick cooking spray; set aside.

◆ In a medium saucepan set over low heat melt the butter. Add the marshmallows; mix to coat. Continue to cook and stir until the marshmallows are completely melted and the mixture is well blended. Remove from heat and stir in the vanilla. Mix in the cereal and toffee bars, stirring to coat well.

◆ Using a wooden spoon, press cereal mixture firmly into prepared muffin tins to form; gently press an indentation into each tassie using the back of a rounded tablespoon. Cool at least 30 minutes; remove from pans.

◆ Fill each indentation with caramel apple dip. Refrigerate 30 minutes. Store in the refrigerator. ◆ Makes 24 tassies.

Shaped Cookies

Brandied Fruitcake Cookies

Here's an easily assembled cookie with all of the rich flavor, but none of the fuss, of homemade fruitcake.

1	**9-ounce package condensed mincemeat, finely crumbled (e.g., None Such® brand)**
2	**cups vanilla wafer crumbs**
1	**cup sweetened flake coconut**
5	**tablespoons brandy, bourbon, or rum**
3	**tablespoons light corn syrup**
1²/₃	**cups powdered sugar, divided use**

◆ Line two cookie sheets with wax paper.

◆ In a large bowl combine the mincemeat, crumbs, coconut, brandy, corn syrup, and 1 cup powdered sugar until well blended. Cover and chill 4 hours or as long as overnight.

◆ Place remaining ²/₃ cup powdered sugar in a shallow dish or pie plate. Roll heaping teaspoonfuls of cookie mixture into 1-inch balls. Roll in powdered sugar to coat evenly. Place on prepared sheets. Chill at least 1 day in airtight container to blend flavors. ◆ Makes about 48 cookies.

Shaped Cookies

Lemon Curd Tassies

A double dose of lemon—both zest in the cookie and a lemon curd filling—means these are must-makes on hot, sultry summer days. For a triple lemon experience, serve with tall glasses of ice-cold lemonade.

¹/₄	cup (¹/₂ stick) butter
1	10-ounce package miniature marshmallows
1¹/₄	cups jarred lemon crud
1	teaspoon vanilla extract
1	tablespoon grated lemon zest
7	cups crisp rice cereal

◆ Lightly spray the cups of two 12-count muffin tins; set aside.

◆ In a medium saucepan set over low heat melt the butter. Add the marshmallows; mix to coat. Continue to cook and stir until the marshmallows are completely melted and the mixture is well blended. Remove from heat and stir in the vanilla and lemon zest. Mix in the cereal, stirring to coat well.

◆ Press cereal mixture firmly into prepared muffin tins with a wooden spoon; gently press an indentation into each tassie using the back of a rounded tablespoon. Cool at least 30 minutes; remove from pans.

◆ Fill each indentation with lemon curd. Refrigerate 30 minutes. Store in the refrigerator. ◆ Makes 24 tassies.

Shaped Cookies

Rocky Road Slices

Part cookie, part candy, these rocky road slices make a yummy special occasion treat for kids of all ages.

1	cup semisweet chocolate chips
2	tablespoons ($^1/_4$ stick) butter
1	14-ounce can sweetened condensed milk
3	cups graham cracker crumbs
3	cups miniature marshmallows
$1^1/_2$	cups finely chopped peanuts

◆ Set aside two 20-inch pieces of wax paper.

◆ In heavy saucepan set over low heat melt the chocolate chips and butter with the condensed milk, stirring until blended and smooth.

◆ In a large bowl combine the graham cracker crumbs and marshmallows; stir in the chocolate mixture. Divide mixture in half. Place each portion on a piece of the prepared wax paper; let stand 10 minutes.

◆ Using the wax paper as an aid, shape each portion into a 12-inch log. Place the peanuts on a flat surface covered with wax paper. Roll each log in nuts. Wrap each log tightly; chill for 2 hours or until firm. Remove paper; cut each log into 15 slices. Store covered in refrigerator. ◆ Makes 30 slices.

Shaped Cookies
ROCKY ROAD SLICES

Down Island Coconut Lime Cookies

Bursting with the tropical flavors of ginger, rum, lime, and coconut, these are definitely cookies for summer days when the livin'—and the cookie-making—should be easy.

1	7-ounce bag sweetened flake coconut
1	12-ounce package vanilla wafers, finely crushed
2	cups sifted powdered sugar
2	teaspoons rum flavored extract
1$^1/_2$	teaspoons ground ginger
1	6-ounce can frozen limeade concentrate, thawed and undiluted

◆ Place the coconut in a shallow dish or pie plate; set aside momentarily.

◆ In a medium bowl combine the vanilla wafer crumbs, powdered sugar, rum extract, ginger, and enough of the limeade concentrate to make the mixture stick together; mix well.

◆ Form the mixture into $^1/_2$-inch balls. Roll balls in the coconut to coat, pressing gently to adhere. Store in covered containers between layers of wax paper. Chill 1 day before serving. ◆ Makes about 60 cookies.

Shaped Cookies

Cereal Bars

PB & J Bites

Here's a delectable cookie—based on the tried-and-true peanut butter and jelly sandwich—that will bring you all of the joy and fulfillment you expect from a homemade cookie.

3	cups miniature marshmallows
$1/2$	cup (1 stick) butter
1	cup plus $1^1/2$ tablespoons creamy or crunchy peanut butter, divided use
$4^1/2$	cups crisp rice cereal
$2/3$	cup strawberry jam, stirred to loosen
$2/3$	cup milk chocolate chips
1	tablespoon vegetable shortening

◆ Line an 11x7x2-inch pan with foil (see page 12). Lightly coat foil with nonstick cooking spray.

◆ In a large saucepan set over low heat melt the marshmallows, butter, and 1 cup peanut butter, stirring until blended and smooth. Remove from heat and stir in cereal until well coated.

◆ Turn mixture into prepared pan. Using a square of wax paper or moist fingers, press into prepared pan. Immediately spread strawberry jam over warm cookie base. Set aside momentarily.

◆ In a small saucepan set over low heat melt the chocolate chips, shortening, and remaining $1^1/2$ tablespoons peanut butter, stirring until blended and smooth. Gently spoon and spread mixture over jam layer.

◆ Loosely cover bars with plastic wrap and refrigerate 2 hours or until firm. Cut into 32 pieces. Store in covered containers between layers of wax paper. ◆ Makes 32 "bites."

Crispy Rice Treats

It's a good idea to have a few no-nonsense recipes in any cookie collection, and crispy rice treats hit the mark. Everyone loves them, almost anyone can make them, and they can be enhanced in multiple ways with myriad flavors. A short list of variations follows the master recipe here, but you can let your imagine run wild with combinations of your own design.

3	tablespoons butter
4	cups miniature marshmallows or 1 7-ounce jar marshmallow creme
6	cups crisp rice cereal

◆ Lightly spray a 13x9x2-inch baking pan with nonstick cooking spray; set aside.

◆ Melt the butter in a large saucepan set over low heat. Add marshmallows or marshmallow creme and stir with a wooden spoon until completely melted. Remove from heat. Add the cereal, stirring until all of the cereal is well coated.

◆ Using a large square of wax paper, press mixture evenly into prepared pan. Cool completely. Cut into 2-inch squares. Store in covered containers between layers of wax paper. ◆ Makes 24 squares.

Variations:
Peanut Butter Crispy Treats: Prepare as directed above but stir $1/2$ cup creamy peanut butter into the marshmallow-butter mixture before adding the cereal.

Cocoa Crispy Treats: Prepare as directed above but use cocoa-flavored crisp rice cereal in place of regular crisp rice cereal.

Cereal Bars
CRISPY RICE TREATS

"Pick Your Stir-In" Crispy Rice Treats: Prepare as directed above but stir in 1 cup of any of the following when adding the cereal: miniature semisweet chocolate chips, chopped dried fruit, dried cranberries, raisins, chopped nuts, toffee baking bits, or sweetened flake coconut.

Chocolate Mint Chip Treats: Prepare as directed above but stir in 1 teaspoon peppermint extract to the marshmallow-butter mixture. Add 1 cup miniature semisweet chocolate chips along with the cereal.

Citrus Treats: Prepare as directed above but stir in 1 tablespoon freshly grated lemon, lime, or orange zest to the marshmallow-butter mixture before adding the cereal.

Almond Lover's Treats: Prepare as directed above but stir in $3/4$ teaspoon almond extract to the marshmallow-butter mixture. Add 1 cup coarsely chopped honey-roasted almonds along with the cereal.

Cereal Bars

Scotchie-Toffee Treats

When you're ready to make some treats for a Fourth of July gathering or for winter holiday giving, turn to this page—you won't want to go through any of the holidays without them.

3	tablespoons butter
1	10-ounce package regular marshmallows or miniature marshmallows
3	tablespoons dry butterscotch instant pudding and pie mix
6	cups crisp rice cereal
4	milk chocolate–covered English toffee candy bars, chopped

◆ Lightly spray a 13x9x2-inch baking pan with nonstick cooking spray; set aside.

◆ In a large saucepan set over low heat melt the butter. Add marshmallows and butterscotch pudding mix; stir with a wooden spoon until completely melted. Remove from heat. Add the cereal and toffee candy bars, stirring until all of the cereal is well coated.

◆ Using a large square of wax paper, press mixture evenly into prepared pan. Cool completely. Cut into 2-inch squares. Store in covered containers between layers of wax paper. ◆ Makes 24 squares.

Cereal Bars

Caramel Mocha Crunch Bars

Caramel and coffee pair perfectly with chocolate. All three taste wonderful when stirred together in these rich bars. If you prefer to skip the nuts, leave them out and add an extra cup of cereal to the mix. And if you prefer milk or semisweet chocolate to white, go ahead and make the switch.

1	14-ounce bag caramels, unwrapped
2	tablespoons butter
2	tablespoons water
2	teaspoons instant espresso or coffee powder
6	cups cocoa-flavored crisp rice cereal
1	cup coarsely chopped roasted, lightly salted cashews or almonds
1	cup white chocolate chips, divided use

◇ Lightly spray a 13x9x2-inch baking pan with nonstick cooking spray; set aside.

◇ In a large microwave-safe mixing bowl microwave the caramels, butter, water, and espresso powder on high for 3 minutes or until melted and smooth, stirring after each minute.

◇ Add the cereal and nuts. Stir until well coated. Add $1/2$ cup white chocolate chips, stirring until combined.

◇ Using a large piece of wax paper, press mixture evenly into prepared pan. Let stand about 2 minutes. Sprinkle the remaining white chocolate chips over the mixture. Using wax paper, press the chips evenly into the bars. Cut into large bars when cool. Store in covered containers between layers of wax paper. ◇ Makes 24 bars.

Cereal Bars
CARAMEL MOCHA CRUNCH BARS

Coconut Lime Crispies

Who would have thought that crispy rice treats could be transformed into a tropical taste sensation with just a few simple stir-ins? Whip up a batch—the proof of these crispies is in the tasting.

$^1/_4$	cup ($^1/_2$ stick) butter
4	cups miniature marshmallows
1	tablespoon grated lime zest
1	teaspoon ground ginger
5	cups crisp rice cereal
1 $^1/_2$	cups sweetened flake coconut
$^1/_2$	cup coarsely chopped roasted, lightly salted macadamia nuts (optional)

◆ Lightly spray a 9x9x2-inch square baking pan with nonstick cooking spray; set aside.

◆ Melt the butter in a large saucepan set over low heat. Add the marshmallows; stir until completely melted. Remove from heat and stir in the lime zest and ginger.

◆ Add the cereal, coconut, and nuts, if desired. Stir until well coated.

◆ Using wax paper, press mixture evenly into prepared pan. Cool in refrigerator about 30 minutes. Cut into 12 bars. Store in covered containers between layers of wax paper. ◆ Makes 12 big bars.

Cereal Bars

Chewy Healthnut Raisin Bars

You'll never buy overpriced cereal bars from the supermarket again once you taste these chewy bars, which are equally loaded with great taste and good health.

2	cups 100 percent bran cereal (e.g., All-Bran® cereal, not bran flakes)
³/₄	cup raisins or dried cranberries
¹/₂	cup chopped roasted nuts or roasted, shelled sunflower seeds
1	tablespoon butter
¹/₂	cup honey
¹/₄	cup creamy peanut butter
1	teaspoon vanilla extract
¹/₂	teaspoon ground cinnamon

◆ Lightly spray a 9x9x2-inch square baking pan with nonstick cooking spray; set aside.

◆ In a large bowl stir together the cereal, raisins, and nuts. Set aside.

◆ In a medium saucepan, combine the butter, honey, and peanut butter over medium heat, stirring until mixture is melted and blended. Remove from heat. Stir in vanilla, cinnamon, and cereal mixture until well blended.

◆ Using wax paper, press mixture evenly into prepared pan. Cool completely. Cut into bars. Store in covered containers between layers of wax paper. ◆ Makes 16 bars.

Cereal Bars

Chewy Date Squares

An old-fashioned flavor gives these squares broad appeal. The amount of water is not set in stone given that some dates are drier than others—so add more water, by the teaspoonful, as needed.

3	tablespoons butter
1	cup chopped pitted dates
1	tablespoon water
4	tablespoons packed brown sugar, divided use
3	tablespoons coarsely chopped pecans or walnuts
$^1/_2$	cup light corn syrup
1	teaspoon vanilla extract
6	cups multigrain or bran flakes cereal, crushed to 4 cups

◆ Lightly spray a 9x9x2-inch square baking pan with nonstick cooking spray; set aside.

◆ In a medium saucepan combine the butter, dates, water, and 3 tablespoons of the brown sugar. Cook over medium heat, stirring constantly until mixture is the consistency of soft paste. Remove from heat. Stir in the nuts; set aside.

◆ In a large saucepan heat the corn syrup and the remaining 1 tablespoon brown sugar over medium heat, stirring constantly until mixture comes to a rolling boil. Boil 1 minute. Remove from heat; stir in vanilla. Add the cereal and mix until well blended.

◆ Using a square of wax paper, press half the mixture evenly and firmly into prepared pan. Spread evenly with date mixture. Press remaining cereal mixture evenly over date layer, pressing lightly. Cool completely. Cut into 16 bars. Store in covered containers between layers of wax paper. ◆ Makes 16 bars.

Cereal Bars

CHEWY DATE SQUARES

Chewy Cinnamon Roll Bars

The taste of a rich, chewy caramel cinnamon roll is captured in these delicious bars, which can be assembled in minutes.

1	**14-ounce can sweetened condensed milk**
1³/₄	**cups white chocolate chips**
1	**10-ounce package miniature marshmallows**
2	**teaspoons ground cinnamon**
1	**15-ounce package toasted oat O-shaped cereal (13 cups)**
1	**cup toffee baking bits**

◆ Line a 15x10x1-inch jelly roll pan with foil (see page 12). Lightly coat foil with nonstick cooking spray.

◆ In a large saucepan or Dutch oven set over medium heat cook the condensed milk, white chocolate chips, and marshmallows, stirring constantly, until melted and smooth. Stir in cinnamon, cereal, and toffee bits.

◆ Turn mixture into the prepared pan. Using a square of wax paper or moist fingers, press into pan. Cool 1–2 hours or until firm. Cut into 24 bars. Store in covered containers between layers of wax paper. ◆ Makes 24 big bars.

Salty-Sweet Chewy Popcorn Bars

Whether for snack time, potluck gatherings, or late-night movie-watching, these salty-sweet, caramel popcorn cookies are popular.

8	cups popped popcorn
2	cups honey graham cereal
1	cup candy-coated chocolate pieces (e.g., M & Ms)
1	cup salted pretzel sticks, broken in half
1/2	cup (1 stick) butter
1	cup firmly packed brown sugar
1/2	cup light corn syrup
2	tablespoons all-purpose flour

◆ Lightly spray a 13x9x2-inch baking pan with nonstick cooking spray; set aside.

◆ In a very large bowl combine the popcorn, cereal, candy, and pretzels; set aside.

◆ In a medium saucepan set over medium heat melt the butter. Stir in all remaining ingredients. Continue cooking, stirring occasionally, until mixture comes to a full boil. Boil 1 minute without stirring.

◆ Pour caramel mixture over popcorn mixture; toss with wooden spoon to coat well. With a large square of wax paper, press firmly into prepared pan. Cool completely. Cut into 24 bars. Store in covered containers between layers of wax paper. ◆ Makes 24 big bars.

Cereal Bars

Chocolate Peanut Butter Crisp Rice Bars

Always a favorite with kids, these rich bars belie their short list of ingredients.

2	**cups semisweet chocolate chips**
²/₃	**cup creamy peanut butter**
6	**cups crisp rice cereal**
3	**cups miniature marshmallows**

◇ Lightly spray a 13x9x2-inch baking pan with nonstick cooking spray; set aside.

◇ In a large saucepan melt the chocolate chips and peanut butter over low heat, stirring constantly until smooth. Remove from heat. Stir in cereal and marshmallows.

◇ Using a large square of wax paper, press mixture evenly into prepared pan. Chill in refrigerator about 45 minutes to set. Cut into 18 bars. Store in covered containers between layers of wax paper. ◇ Makes 18 big bars.

Layered Chocolate-Mallow Yummies

Crisp graham crackers compose the foundation of these very yummy bars, which are part s'more, part crispy rice treat, part peanut butter cup candy.

7	graham crackers (whole rectangles)
2$^1/_2$	cups miniature marshmallows
2	cups semisweet chocolate morsels
$^2/_3$	cup light corn syrup
3	tablespoons butter
$^1/_2$	cup crunchy peanut butter
3	cups crisp rice cereal

◆ Lightly spray a 13x9x2-inch baking pan with nonstick cooking spray.

◆ Place six whole pieces graham crackers in single layer in bottom of prepared pan. Cut remaining piece to fit in bottom. Sprinkle marshmallows evenly over crackers; set aside.

◆ In a medium saucepan set over low heat melt the chocolate chips, corn syrup, and butter, stirring constantly until blended and smooth. Remove from heat and stir in peanut butter. Add cereal, mixing until combined.

◆ Immediately spread cereal mixture evenly over marshmallows, using a large square of wax paper to help spread. Cover and refrigerate about 1 hour or until firm. Cut into 36 bars. Store in covered containers between layers of wax paper. ◆ Makes 36 bars.

Cereal Bars

White Christmas Cranberry Mallow Bars

As much as I love it, white chocolate isn't "true" chocolate. Rather, it is a combination of sugar, cocoa butter, and milk solids. Regardless, it is delicious, especially in these pretty, holiday cookies flecked with orange zest and cranberries.

2	**cups white chocolate chips**
2	**tablespoons vegetable shortening**
1	**cup miniature marshmallows**
$^1/_2$	**cup coarsely chopped honey-roasted almonds**
1	**cup chopped dried cranberries**
2	**teaspoons grated orange zest**
2	**cups crisp rice cereal**

◆ Lightly spray an 8x8x2-inch square baking pan with nonstick cooking spray; set aside.

◆ In a medium saucepan set over low heat melt the white chocolate chips and shortening, stirring constantly until smooth. Remove from heat. Stir in the marshmallows, almonds, cranberries, orange zest, and cereal, mixing until well coated.

◆ Spread mixture evenly into prepared pan. Refrigerate about 1 hour until set. Cut into 24 bars. Store in covered containers between layers of wax paper. ◆ Makes 24 small bars.

Cereal Bars

Frosted Chocolate Candy Bar Chews

When the season of potlucks, parties, and pitch-ins rolls around, we all need a few terrific, foolproof recipes to prepare and take in short order. These candy bar-like cookies fit the bill, deliciously.

1	cup light corn syrup
1	cup packed light brown sugar
1	cup peanut butter
8	cups crisp rice cereal
1	cup milk chocolate chips
1	cup butterscotch chips

◆ Lightly spray a 13x9x2-inch baking pan with nonstick cooking spray; set aside.

◆ Place corn syrup and brown sugar into a medium-size saucepan. Stir to combine. Cook over medium heat, stirring frequently, until mixture begins to bubble. Remove from heat. Stir in peanut butter.

◆ Add the cereal and stir until evenly coated. With a large square of wax paper, press mixture evenly and firmly in bottom of prepared pan. Cool.

◆ Melt chocolate and butterscotch chips together in small saucepan over very low heat, stirring constantly. Spread evenly over cereal mixture. Cool completely. Cut into 36 bars. Store in covered containers between layers of wax paper. ◆ Makes 36 bars.

Cereal Bars

Peanut-Buttercream Crunch Bars

A thick layer of vanilla buttercream gets sandwiched between a crispy peanut butter cookie base and a white chocolate fudge topping in these incredible bars.

1	cup sugar
1	cup light corn syrup
2	cups creamy peanut butter
3	cups crisp rice cereal
3	cups cornflakes
1$^1/_4$	cups (2$^1/_2$ sticks) butter, divided use
4	cups sifted powdered sugar
2	4-serving-size packages instant vanilla pudding mix
2–4	tablespoons milk
1	12-ounce package white chocolate chips (2 cups)

◆ Lightly spray a 15x10x1-inch jelly roll pan with nonstick cooking spray; set aside.

◆ In a large saucepan heat the sugar and corn syrup just until mixture boils on the edge of the pan. Cook and stir 1 minute more; remove from heat. Stir in peanut butter until melted and blended. Stir in rice cereal and cornflakes until coated. With a large square of wax paper, press into bottom of prepared pan; set aside.

◆ In a medium saucepan, melt $^3/_4$ cup (1$^1/_2$ sticks) of the butter. Stir in powdered sugar, vanilla pudding mixes, and enough of the milk to make spreading consistency. Spread over cereal layer; set aside.

◆ In a small saucepan, heat the white chocolate chips and remaining $^1/_2$ cup butter over low heat, stirring constantly until melted. Spread over pudding layer. Cover and chill in the refrigerator for at least 1 hour or until set. Cut into 64 bars. Store in covered containers between layers of wax paper. ◆ Makes 64 bars.

Cereal Bars

Lemon Layered Bars

Smooth and cool with the flavor of lemon, these layered citrus bars are home-run hot weather fare.

12	tablespoons (1^1/$_2$ stick) butter, softened, divided use
4	1-ounce squares white chocolate, divided use
1^1/$_2$	tablespoons pasteurized egg product (e.g., Egg Beaters)
1	cup quick-cooking oats, uncooked
1^1/$_2$	cups sweetened flake coconut
^{1}/$_2$	cup finely chopped almonds
1	teaspoon vanilla extract
2^1/$_2$	cups powdered sugar, divided use
2	teaspoons grated lemon zest
2^1/$_2$	tablespoons lemon juice

◇ Lightly spray a 9x9x2-inch pan with nonstick cooking spray; set aside.

◇ In a saucepan melt 8 tablespoons (1 stick) of the butter with 2 squares of the white chocolate until smooth. Remove from heat and stir in the egg product, oats, coconut, almonds, vanilla, and ^{1}/$_2$ cup of the powdered sugar. With a large square of wax paper, press mixture into prepared pan. Chill for 1 hour.

◇ In a medium bowl blend the remaining 2 cups powdered sugar with the lemon zest, lemon juice, and 3 tablespoons of the remaining softened butter, mixing until it has an icing-like consistency. Spread lemon mixture over the oat mixture in the pan. Chill for 30 minutes.

◇ In a small saucepan melt the remaining 1 tablespoon butter with the remaining 2 squares white chocolate. Spread over the top of the bars. Chill 1 hour to set chocolate. Cut into 16 bars. Store in covered containers between layers of wax paper. ◇ Makes 16 squares.

Cereal Bars
LEMON LAYERED BARS

Peanut Butterscotch Fudge Bars

Loaded with a winning combination of butterscotch, peanut butter, and marshmallows, these incredible treats will tempt one and all.

3$^1/_2$	tablespoons butter, divided use
4	cups miniature marshmallows, divided use
1	cup creamy peanut butter, divided use
3	cups toasted rice cereal
$^2/_3$	cup canned evaporated milk
1$^1/_2$	cups sugar
1	cup butterscotch baking chips
$^3/_4$	cup creamy peanut butter
1	teaspoon vanilla extract
$^1/_4$	cup cocktail peanuts, chopped

◇ Lightly spray a 13x9x2-inch baking pan with nonstick cooking spray; set aside.

◇ In a medium saucepan set over low heat melt 1$^1/_2$ tablespoons of the butter. Add 2 cups marshmallows and $^1/_4$ cup peanut butter and stir until melted and smooth. Remove from heat. Add cereal and stir until blended. With a large square of wax paper, press mixture into bottom of prepared pan.

◇ In a medium saucepan combine the evaporated milk, sugar, and remaining 2 tablespoons butter. Bring to a boil over medium heat, stirring constantly. Continue to boil, stirring constantly, for 4–5 minutes. Remove from heat.

◇ Add the remaining 2 cups marshmallows, butterscotch chips, vanilla, and remaining $^3/_4$ cup peanut butter to the hot milk mixture; stir vigorously for 1 minute or until marshmallows and chips are completely melted. Pour and spread mixture over prepared crust. Sprinkle with peanuts. Refrigerate 1 hour to set the bars. Cut into 36 bars. Store in covered containers between layers of wax paper. ◇ Makes 36 bars.

Cereal Bars

Baklava Crispy Bars

Baklava is a butter-rich, layered Greek pastry, filled with spices, lemon, honey and nuts. While this crispy, no-bake bar is a significant departure from the original in terms of form, it captures the much beloved combination of flavors.

2	tablespoons butter
$^1/_3$	cup honey
4	cups miniature marshmallows
$1^1/_2$	teaspoons ground cinnamon
1	tablespoon grated lemon zest
6	cups oats and honey crispy cereal
1	cup chopped walnuts

◆ Lightly spray a 13x9x2-inch baking pan with nonstick cooking spray; set aside.

◆ In a large saucepan or Dutch oven set over low heat melt the butter with the honey, stirring until blended. Add the marshmallows, cinnamon, and lemon zest; cook and stir until melted and blended.

◆ Add the cereal and walnuts; mix well. With a large square of wax paper, press cereal mixture firmly into prepared pan. Cool completely. Cut into 24 bars. Store in covered containers between layers of wax paper. ◆ Makes 24 big bars.

Cereal Bars

High-Energy Dried Fruit Bars

One thing's for certain—you'll expend very little energy making these power-packed treats, which stir together in no time. For a chocolate twist, substitute an equal amount of chocolate-hazelnut spread for the peanut butter.

4	**cups wheat & barley nugget cereal (e.g., Grape Nuts®)**
1	**cup dried fruit, such as raisins, cranberries, cherries, or dried fruit bits**
1	**cup honey**
1	**cup packed light brown sugar**
³/₄	**cup creamy peanut butter**

◆ Lightly spray a 13x9x2-inch baking pan with nonstick cooking spray; set aside.

◆ Place cereal and fruit in a large bowl; set aside.

◆ In a medium saucepan mix the honey, brown sugar, and peanut butter. Bring to a boil over medium-low heat, stirring occasionally. Pour peanut butter mixture over cereal and fruit mixture, stirring until blended.

◆ With a large square of wax paper, press mixture firmly into prepared pan. Cool completely. Cut into 30 bars. Wrap bars individually with plastic wrap. Store in tightly covered container. ◆ Makes 30 bars.

Cereal Bars

Ginger Bars with Lemon Frosting

When it's high time for teatime, head for this recipe. The bite of ginger and brightness of lemon have a natural affinity that is always satisfying.

¹/₂	cup (1 stick) plus 3 tablespoons butter, divided use
¹/₂	cup packed dark brown sugar
¹/₂	cup unsweetened canned evaporated milk
2¹/₄	teaspoons ground ginger
2	teaspoons vanilla extract
2	cups uncooked quick oats
¹/₂	cup toasted wheat germ
1	cup sweetened flake coconut
¹/₃	cup white chocolate chips
1	3-ounce package cream cheese, softened
1	teaspoon grated lemon zest
1¹/₂	teaspoons lemon juice
2¹/₄	cups powdered sugar

◇ Lightly spray a 9x9x2-inch square baking pan with nonstick cooking spray; set aside.

◇ In a medium-size saucepan melt ¹/₂ cup (1 stick) of the butter. Add the brown sugar and evaporated milk. Cook and stir until over medium heat until sugar is dissolved. Remove from the heat and add the ginger, vanilla, oats, wheat germ, and coconut; mix well. Spread the mixture into a prepared pan with a wooden spoon; set aside.

◇ In a small saucepan set over low heat melt the remaining 3 tablespoons butter with the white chocolate chips. Transfer mixture to a medium bowl and add the cream cheese, lemon zest, and lemon juice. Beat with an electric mixer set

Cereal Bars

on medium-high speed until blended. Gradually beat in powdered sugar until mixture reaches spreading consistency.

◆ Spread the cream cheese mixture over the bars. Refrigerate until firm. Cut into 16 bars. Store in covered containers between layers of wax paper. ◆ Makes 16 bars.

Almond Squares with Dried Cherries

I don't like to turn on the oven in the sweltering heat, but sometimes I want to bypass baking in the fall, too, especially when I'm pressed for time. These almond-accented bars, balanced with the tart-sweet taste of dried cherries, are a perfect solution.

3	cups bite-sized pieces shredded wheat cereal, coarsely crushed
$3/4$	cup dried tart cherries or dried cranberries
$1/2$	cup chopped, lightly salted roasted almonds
$1/2$	cup light corn syrup or honey
$1/2$	cup firmly packed brown sugar
$1/2$	cup almond butter
1	teaspoon almond extract

◆ Lightly spray an 8x8x2-inch square baking pan with nonstick cooking spray; set aside.

◆ Place cereal, cherries, and almonds in a large bowl; set aside.

◆ In a medium saucepan mix the corn syrup, brown sugar, and almond butter. Bring to a boil over medium heat, stirring occasionally. Remove from heat and stir in almond extract.

◆ Pour almond butter mixture over cereal mixture, stirring until blended.

◆ With a large square of wax paper, press firmly into prepared pan. Cool completely. Cut into 24 small squares. Store in covered containers between layers of wax paper. ◆ Makes 24 squares.

Cereal Bars

Fluffernutter Sandwich Bars

The fluffernutter sandwich—peanut butter and marshmallow fluff, sandwiched between two slices of white bread—was invented back in 1961 by Durkee-Mower, Inc., the company that developed the first version of marshmallow fluff. Here it is reinvented in cookie form, with even more peanut butter and more marshmallow.

$^1/_4$	cup ($^1/_2$ stick) butter
1	10-ounce package miniature marshmallows
1	16-ounce box honey and nut flakes & clusters cereal
$^1/_2$	cup creamy peanut butter
$^2/_3$	cup jarred marshmallow fluff or creme

◆ Line a 15x10x1-inch pan with foil; lightly spray foil with nonstick cooking spray. Set aside.

◆ In large saucepan on low heat melt the butter. Add miniature marshmallows; cook until melted, stirring constantly. Remove from heat. Stir in cereal, mixing until blended. With a large square of wax paper, press firmly into prepared pan. Cool completely.

◆ Remove formed cereal mixture from pan by turning pan upside down on cutting board. Remove pan and peel off foil. Cut rectangle in half lengthwise. Spread one half with peanut butter; spread other half with marshmallow creme. Stack halves, peanut butter and marshmallow creme sides together, to form sandwich.

◆ Cut into 24 bars. Store in covered containers between layers of wax paper. ◆ Makes 24 bars.

Cereal Bars

Maple Cranberry Crunch Bars

People often ask, "What's your favorite recipe in the book?" The answer to the question is never easy, but for this collection, these simple bars are it. I love the contrast of the maple with the tart cranberries and crunchy pecans. And although the flavors are fitting for cool autumn days and holiday gatherings, you'll find that these gems are popular year-round.

$^1/_3$	cup pure maple syrup
2	tablespoons ($^1/_4$ stick) butter
4	cups miniature marshmallows
$1^1/_2$	teaspoons maple-flavored extract (optional)
6	cups honey and nut flakes & clusters cereal
1	cup dried cranberries
1	cup chopped pecans

◆ Lightly spray a 13x9x2-inch baking pan with nonstick cooking spray; set aside.

◆ In a large saucepan set over low heat cook the maple syrup and butter, stirring until butter is melted and mixture is bubbly. Add marshmallows; cook and stir until marshmallows are melted. Remove from heat and mix in maple extract, cereal, cranberries, and pecans; stir to coat well.

◆ With a large square of wax paper, press firmly into prepared pan. Cool completely. Cut into 24 bars. Store in covered containers between layers of wax paper. ◆ Makes 24 bars.

Cereal Bars

Maui-Wowie Macadamia Bars

This is a beautifully simple yet very delicious cookie with a big "wow" factor. A little bit crunchy, a little bit chewy, the perfect level of sweetness and lots of big tropical flavors make it ideal summer-dessert fare.

¹/₃	**cup honey**
2	**tablespoons butter**
2	**teaspoons ground ginger**
4	**cups miniature marshmallows**
2	**teaspoons grated lime zest**
6	**cups honey and nut flakes & clusters cereal**
1	**cup dried tropical fruit bits**
1	**cup chopped, lightly salted roasted macadamia nuts**

◆ Lightly spray a 13x9x2-inch baking pan with nonstick cooking spray; set aside.

◆ In a large saucepan set over low heat cook and stir the honey and butter until butter is melted and mixture is bubbly. Add the ginger, marshmallows, and lime zest. Cook and stir until marshmallows are melted and mixture is blended. Remove from heat and mix in cereal, tropical fruit bits, and macadamia nuts; stir to coat well.

◆ With a large square of wax paper, press firmly into prepared pan. Cool completely. Cut into 24 bars. Store in covered containers between layers of wax paper. ◆ Makes 24 bars.

Banana Bars

These delicious confections are just as delightful eaten during a midmorning coffee break as they are devoured as a midnight snack. If you are not a coconut fan, leave it out and substitute an extra ¹/₂ cup of cereal in its place.

¹/₄	cup (¹/₂ stick) butter
1	10-ounce bag marshmallows
6	cups crisp rice cereal
1	cup coarsely crushed dried banana chips
1	cup coarsely chopped, lightly salted roasted cashews, peanuts, or macadamia nuts
¹/₂	cup sweetened flake coconut

◆ Lightly spray a 13x9x2-inch baking pan with nonstick cooking spray; set aside.

◆ In large saucepan or Dutch oven set over medium heat melt the butter. Add the marshmallows. Cook and stir until marshmallows are melted. Remove from heat.

◆ Stir in cereal, banana chips, nuts, and coconut until evenly coated. With a large square of wax paper, press into prepared pan evenly. Cool 30 minutes. Cut into 36 bars. Store in covered containers between layers of wax paper. ◆ Makes 36 bars.

Baker's Note: To easily crush banana chips, place in a large, resealable plastic bag. Place on a flat surface and use a rolling pin or mallet to crush the chips.

Cereal Bars
BANANA BARS

Pineapple-Orange Snack Bars

Look for dried pineapple slices in the bulk foods section at the grocery store or check out the section of the store where raisins are shelved. In the latter section, the dried pineapple is more likely to be found prechopped.

2	tablespoons ($^1/_4$ stick) butter
$^1/_4$	cup sugar
$^1/_4$	cup honey
$2^1/_2$	teaspoons grated orange zest
$1^1/_2$	cups honey nut cornflakes cereal
1	cup chopped dried pineapple (about 4 ounces)
$^1/_2$	cup sliced almonds

◆ Lightly spray an 8x8x2-inch square baking pan with nonstick cooking spray; set aside.

◆ In a medium saucepan combine the butter, sugar, and honey. Bring to boil over medium heat, stirring constantly. Reduce heat and simmer 3 minutes, stirring constantly. Remove from heat. Carefully stir in orange zest.

◆ Add the cereal, pineapple, and almonds to syrup mixture, mixing until thoroughly coated. With a large square of wax paper, press into prepared pan. Let stand until firm. Cut into 12 bars. Store in covered containers between layers of wax paper. ◆ Makes 12 bars.

Cereal Bars

Chewy Apricot Granola Bars

At my house, these granola bars are standard fare, perfect for snacks, lunch bags, breakfast on the run, and late-night munching. They can be varied in multiple ways by changing out the type of dried fruit (e.g., cranberries, cherries, tropical fruit mixes, and raisins), using baking chips in place of the dried fruit (e.g., chocolate chips, carob chips, or toffee baking bits), and using different types of nuts and seeds in place of the sunflower seeds (roasted pumpkin seeds—also known as pepitas—are a delicious option).

1	10-ounce bag miniature marshmallows
$1/4$	cup ($1/2$ stick) butter
$3^3/4$	cups granola with almonds
$1^1/2$	cups crisp rice cereal
1	cup chopped dried apricots
$1/2$	cup roasted, lightly salted sunflower seeds

◆ Line a 13x9x2-inch pan with foil (see page 12). Lightly spray foil with nonstick cooking spray; set aside.

◆ In a large saucepan combine the marshmallows and butter. Cook and stir mixture until the marshmallows are melted. Remove from heat.

◆ Stir in granola, cereal, apricots, and sunflower seeds until well blended. With a large square of wax paper, press mixture into the prepared pan. Cool completely. Use the foil overhang to lift bars out of pan. Peel off foil. Cut into 24 bars. Store in covered containers between layers of wax paper. ◆ Makes 24 big bars.

Cereal Bars

Black Forest Bites

These cookies are based on the flavors of a far more complicated chocolate and cherry torte called Schwarzwalder Kirschtorte. It hails from the Black Forest region of Germany—hence the shortened name, Black Forest Torte. The classic flavor combination still holds tremendous appeal when simplified into these no-bake petites.

2	cups semisweet chocolate chips
2	tablespoons vegetable shortening
1	cup miniature marshmallows
$^1/_2$	teaspoon almond extract
$^2/_3$	cup dried cherries or cranberries
2	cups crisp rice cereal

◆ Lightly spray an 8x8x2-inch square baking pan with nonstick cooking spray; set aside.

◆ In a medium saucepan place the chocolate chips and shortening. Stir over low heat until chips are melted and mixture is smooth. Remove from heat and stir in the marshmallows, almond extract, cherries, and cereal. Mix well.

◆ Using a large square of wax paper, press and spread mixture into the prepared pan. Chill until set. Cut into 24 small squares. Store in covered containers between layers of wax paper. ◆ Makes 24 "bites."

Holiday Honey-Gumdrop Bars

These showy cookies feature the flavors and the colors of Christmas with very little effort.

1	13-ounce package (about 8 cups) honey graham cereal squares
2	cups red and green small spice drops
2	cups white chocolate chips or vanilla baking chips
$^1/_3$	cup butter
$^1/_4$	cup honey
1	10-ounce package miniature marshmallows
1	teaspoon ground ginger
1	teaspoon vanilla extract

◆ Lightly spray a 13x9x2-inch square baking pan with nonstick cooking spray; set aside.

◆ Lightly spray a large bowl with nonstick cooking spray. Combine the cereal and spice drops in the bowl; set aside.

◆ In a large saucepan melt the white chocolate chips with the butter and honey over low heat, stirring until melted and smooth. Add the marshmallows and cook, stirring constantly, until melted and smooth. Remove from heat and stir in the ground ginger and vanilla.

◆ Pour the marshmallow mixture over the cereal mixture in bowl, folding gently to mix. Turn into sprayed pan. With large square of wax paper, press and spread mixture evenly in pan. Cool 30 minutes. Cut into 36 bars. Store in covered containers between layers of wax paper. ◆ Makes 36 bars.

Cereal Bars

HOLIDAY HONEY-GUMDROP BARS

Dried Apple-Almond Butter Bars

To transform ordinary oat cereal into a tasty, homespun treat, hold the baking and try making these apple-almond bars instead.

$^1/_2$	cup packed light brown sugar
$^1/_2$	cup light corn syrup
$^1/_2$	cup almond butter (crunchy peanut butter may be substituted)
$^1/_2$	teaspoon cinnamon
4	cups honey-nut O-shape oat cereal
1	cup chopped dried apples

❖ Lightly spray an 8x8x2-inch baking pan with nonstick cooking spray; set aside.

❖ In a large saucepan or Dutch oven combine the brown sugar and corn syrup. Cook over medium heat, stirring constantly, until mixture boils. Remove from heat and stir in almond butter and cinnamon. Add cereal and dried apples, stirring until evenly coated.

❖ Press hot cereal mixture evenly into prepared pan with a wooden spoon. Cool completely. Cut into 16 bars. Store in covered containers between layers of wax paper. ❖ Makes 16 bars.

Toffee Squares

When it comes to sweets, my biggest weakness is brown sugar. Hence, toffee bars are definitely favorites on my treat list. This no-bake version comes from the combination of several recipes and lots of trial and error. I think they are as tasty as the ones that take twice as long—or longer—to prepare.

1	cup all-purpose flour
$1/2$	teaspoon baking powder
$1/2$	teaspoon salt
2	cups bran flakes cereal
$3/4$	cup plus 2 tablespoons milk, divided use
1	cup firmly packed dark brown sugar
10	tablespoons ($1^{1}/_4$ sticks) butter, softened, divided use
2	large eggs
$1^{1}/_2$	teaspoons vanilla extract, divided use
2	cups sifted powdered sugar

◆ Lightly spray an 8x8x2-inch microwave-safe baking pan with nonstick cooking spray; set aside.

◆ In a medium bowl mix the flour, baking powder, and salt until blended. Set aside.

◆ In a small mixing bowl combine the cereal and $3/4$ cup milk. Let stand 2–3 minutes or until cereal is softened.

◆ In medium mixing bowl beat the brown sugar and 8 tablespoons (1 stick) butter with an electric mixer set on medium-high speed until light and fluffy. Add the eggs and 1 teaspoon vanilla. Beat well. Stir in the cereal mixture. Add the flour mixture, stirring until well blended.

Cereal Bars
TOFFEE SQUARES

◆ Spread the batter evenly in the prepared pan.

◆ Microwave on high about 10 minutes or until wooden pick inserted near center comes out clean. Rotate every 3 minutes. Remove from microwave. Cool completely.

◆ In a small bowl combine the powdered sugar, remaining 2 tablespoons ($^1/_4$ stick) butter, remaining 2 tablespoons milk, and remaining $^1/_2$ teaspoon vanilla with an electric mixer set on low speed until blended and smooth. Spread frosting evenly over cooled bars. Cut into 16 bars. Store in covered containers between layers of wax paper. ◆ Makes 16 bars.

Cereal Bars
TOFFEE SQUARES

Almond Butterscotch Squares

Regardless of your feelings about nuts in desserts, you're sure to love these sweet treats.

2	cups butterscotch baking chips
2	tablespoons vegetable shortening
$^1/_2$	teaspoon almond extract
1	cup miniature marshmallows
1	cup coarsely chopped honey-roasted almonds
2	cups crisp rice cereal

◆ Lightly spray an 8x8x2-inch square baking pan with nonstick cooking spray; set aside.

◆ In a medium saucepan place the butterscotch chips and shortening. Stir over low heat until chips are melted and mixture is smooth. Remove from heat; stir in the almond extract, marshmallows, almonds, and cereal. Mix well.

◆ Spread mixture into the prepared pan with a wooden spoon. Chill until set. Cut into 24 small squares. Store in covered containers between layers of wax paper. ◆ Makes 24 squares.

Cereal Bars

Karma Krunch Bars

Here's an innovative twist on the no-bake cookie. Bright with the flavor of citrus, sweet with honey and tropical fruit, and peppery with ginger, they're sure to be favorites at your next picnic pitch-in.

2	tablespoons butter
1/3	cup honey
4	cups miniature marshmallows
2	teaspoons ground ginger
6	cups oats and honey crispy cereal
1	cup dried tropical fruit bits or other dried fruit of choice
3/4	cup roasted, lightly salted sunflower seeds
1	tablespoon grated lemon or lime zest

◆ Lightly spray a 13x9x2-inch baking pan with nonstick cooking spray; set aside.

◆ In a large saucepan or Dutch oven melt the butter with the honey over low heat, stirring until blended. Add the marshmallows and ginger. Cook and stir until marshmallows are melted and mixture is blended.

◆ Add the cereal, dried fruit, sunflower seeds, and zest to marshmallow mixture; mix well. With a large square of wax paper, press cereal mixture firmly into prepared pan. Cool completely. Cut into 24 bars. Store in covered containers between layers of wax paper. ◆ Makes 24 bars.

Cereal Bars

Chocolate Trail Blazer Bars

Packaged energy bars? Never again, once you taste these delicious bars. They will power you through the most hectic of days.

3	1-ounce squares unsweetened chocolate, coarsely chopped
$^1/_4$	cup creamy or crunchy-style peanut butter
1	14-ounce can sweetened condensed milk
1	teaspoon vanilla extract
$4^1/_2$	cups granola cereal
$1^1/_3$	cups sweetened flake coconut

◆ Lightly spray a 13x9x2-inch baking pan with nonstick cooking spray; set aside.

◆ In a large saucepan or Dutch oven melt the chocolate and peanut butter with the condensed milk over low heat, stirring until blended and smooth.

◆ Remove saucepan from heat. Stir in the vanilla, granola, and coconut until well blended. With a large square of wax paper, press into prepared pan. Chill 1–2 hours or until set. Cut into 24 bars. Store in covered containers between layers of wax paper. ◆ Makes 24 bars.

Cereal Bars

California Dried Fruit & Nut Bars

Dried fruit makes a great, wholesome cookie in short order. Any combination of chopped dried fruit will work here. To avoid the chopping step, look for prechopped dried fruit mixes in the supermarket where raisins are shelved. They are typically packaged in traditional blends (e.g., dried raisins, cranberries, apricots, and plums) or in unusual blends such as tropical fruit medleys.

1/2	cup (1 stick) butter
1/2	cup firmly packed light brown sugar
2	large egg yolks, slightly beaten
1	cup mixed dried fruits, chopped
1	cup lightly salted, coarsely chopped roasted nuts
2	cups crisp rice cereal

◆ Lightly spray a 9x9x2-inch baking pan with nonstick cooking spray; set aside.

◆ In a large nonstick skillet melt the butter. Remove from heat and add the brown sugar and egg yolks. Return to low heat and cook and stir until mixture simmers and thickens slightly. Remove from heat and stir in the dried fruits, nuts, and cereal.

◆ Cool 5 minutes. With a large square of wax paper, firmly press mixture into prepared pan. Cool completely. Cut into 16 bars. Store in covered containers between layers of wax paper. ◆ Makes 16 bars.

Chocolate-Marshmallow Bars

Rich and chewy with marshmallows and two kinds of chips, these cookie bars are worth every gooey bite.

¹/₂	cup (1 stick) butter
2	cups semisweet chocolate chips
1	cup butterscotch baking chips
1	cup creamy peanut butter
4	cups crisp rice cereal
3	cups miniature marshmallows
³/₄	cup chopped walnuts or pecans, skillet toasted and cooled (see page 8) (optional)

◆ Spray a 13x9x2-inch baking pan with nonstick cooking spray; set aside.

◆ In a large saucepan or Dutch oven set over low heat melt the butter, chocolate chips, and butterscotch chips, stirring constantly until melted and smooth. Mix in peanut butter until blended.

◆ Remove the saucepan from the heat. Add the cereal, marshmallows, and nuts, if desired, and toss until well coated.

◆ With a large square of wax paper, press mixture onto bottom of prepared pan. Refrigerate 30 minutes or until firm. Cut into 36 bars. Store in covered containers between layers of wax paper. ◆ Makes 36 bars.

Cereal Bars
CHOCOLATE-MARSHMALLOW BARS

Honey Sesame Crunch Bars

Make lunch extra special by ending it with one of these sweet bars. The honey and sesame add a unique, slightly exotic flavor to the cookie base.

1	cup packed dark brown sugar
$^2/_3$	cup honey
$^1/_2$	cup all-purpose flour
6	tablespoons ($^3/_4$ stick) butter
2	tablespoons toasted sesame oil
$^1/_3$	cup milk
4	cups toasted honey graham cereal squares
3	cups crisp rice cereal
$^1/_4$	cup sesame seeds
1	cup coarsely chopped roasted, salted peanuts or cashews
2	cups white or milk chocolate chips

◆ Lightly spray a 13x9x2-inch baking pan with nonstick cooking spray; set aside.

◆ In a large saucepan or Dutch oven combine the brown sugar, honey, flour, butter, sesame oil, and milk. Cook over medium heat, stirring occasionally, until mixture comes to a full boil. Boil, stirring constantly, for 5 minutes.

◆ Remove saucepan from heat. Add the cereals, sesame seeds, and peanuts, tossing until well coated.

◆ Spread mixture into prepared pan with a wooden spoon. Immediately sprinkle the warm bars with chocolate chips. Cover pan with a cookie sheet and let stand 4 minutes. Spread chocolate chips over bars. Cover and refrigerate 30 minutes or until firm. Store in covered containers between layers of wax paper. Cut into bars. ◆ Makes 36 bars.

Cereal Bars

Chocolate-Chip Oatmeal Bars

Apple pie is often heralded as the favorite American dessert, but a strong case can be made for the chocolate-chip cookie. This no-bake, bar version is a bit of a departure, but it is still scrumptious and rich with the familiar flavors of chocolate, brown sugar, and vanilla.

2¹/₂	cups crisp rice cereal
2	cups quick-cooking oats, uncooked
¹/₂	cup firmly packed dark brown sugar
¹/₂	cup light corn syrup
¹/₂	cup creamy peanut butter
1	teaspoon vanilla extract
1	cup semisweet or milk chocolate chips

◈ Lightly spray an 8x8x2-inch baking pan with nonstick cooking spray; set aside.

◈ Combine the rice cereal and oats in a large bowl; set aside.

◈ In a small saucepan set over medium-high heat bring the brown sugar and corn syrup to a boil, stirring constantly. Remove from heat. Stir in peanut butter and vanilla until blended.

◈ Pour peanut butter mixture over cereal mixture, stirring until coated. Let mixture stand 2 minutes. Stir in the chocolate chips. With a large square of wax paper, press mixture into prepared pan. Cool completely. Cut into 12 bars. Store in covered containers between layers of wax paper. ◈ Makes 12 bars.

Cereal Bars

Chewy Mexican Chocolate Bars

If you are bewitched by a bit of spice in your sweets, than these south-of-the-border cookies are must-makes.

1	cup creamy peanut butter
1	cup light corn syrup
1	cup packed light brown sugar
1	teaspoon ground cinnamon
$^1/_8$	teaspoon ground cloves
$^1/_8$	teaspoon cayenne pepper
$1^1/_4$	cups semisweet chocolate chips, divided use
6	cups cornflakes cereal
1	cup coarsely chopped roasted peanuts

◆ Lightly spray a 13x9x2-inch baking pan with nonstick cooking spray; set aside.

◆ In a large saucepan over medium heat combine the peanut butter, corn syrup, brown sugar, cinnamon, cloves, cayenne, and $^1/_4$ cup of the chocolate chips. Cook, stirring occasionally until smooth. Remove from heat and quickly mix in the cornflakes, peanuts, and remaining 1 cup chocolate chips until mixture is combined.

◆ With a large square of wax paper, press the mixture into the prepared pan with a wooden spoon. Cool completely. Cut into 36 bars. Store in covered containers between layers of wax paper. ◆ Makes 36 bars.

Cereal Bars

Almond Joyful Bars

As the name implies, these simple-to-make—and simply delicious—cookies bear a strong resemblance to the delectable candy with a similar name.

¹/₄	cup (¹/₂ stick) butter
30	large marshmallows
1	teaspoon almond extract
1	cup very coarsely chopped, roasted, lightly salted almonds
2	cups sweetened flake coconut, divided use
3¹/₂	cups cornflakes cereal
1¹/₃	cups milk chocolate chips
1	tablespoon vegetable shortening

◆ Lightly spray a 13x9x2-inch baking pan with nonstick cooking spray; set aside.

◆ In a large saucepan combine the butter and marshmallows. Cook over medium heat, stirring occasionally, until melted and smooth. Stir in the almond extract, almonds, 1 cup of the coconut, and cornflakes. With a large square of wax paper, press into the prepared pan and let sit for 30 minutes.

◆ In a small saucepan set over low heat melt the milk chocolate chips with the vegetable shortening, stirring until melted and smooth. Spread chocolate mixture over cooled bars and sprinkle with remaining 1 cup coconut. Refrigerate 30 minutes to set the chocolate. Cut into 36 bars. Store in covered containers between layers of wax paper. ◆ Makes 36 bars.

Cereal Bars

Chocolate Cinnamon Sandwich Cookies

Eat these sinfully good, intensely chocolate cookies within a few days for the best flavor.

4	cups semisweet chocolate chips, divided use
1	cup creamy peanut butter
2	teaspoons ground cinnamon
8	cups crisp rice cereal
1/4	cup (1/2 stick) butter
1	cup sifted powdered sugar
2	tablespoons milk

◆ Foil-line two 13x9x2-inch baking pans (see page 12); lightly spray with nonstick cooking spray. Set aside.

◆ In a large saucepan set over low heat melt 2 cups of the chocolate chips with the peanut butter, stirring frequently until smooth. Remove from heat and stir in the cinnamon and crisp rice cereal. With a large square of wax paper, press half of the cereal mixture into each of the two prepared pans.

◆ In a medium saucepan melt the butter and remaining 2 cups chocolate chips over low heat, stirring until melted and smooth. Mix in the powdered sugar and milk, stirring until smooth.

◆ Using the foil overhang, remove the cereal mixture from one of the pans; peel off foil. Spread the chocolate mixture evenly over the cereal layer in the other pan. Top with the remaining cereal layer and press down lightly. Cover loosely with plastic wrap and chill for about 1 hour before cutting into 24 bars. Store in covered containers between layers of wax paper. ◆ Makes 24 big bars.

Cereal Bars

Cranberry-Carob Backpacker Bars

Stow one or two of these high-energy bars in your backpack, and you'll be able to climb mountains big and small.

1	cup dried cranberries
1^1/$_2$	cups carob chips or semisweet chocolate chips
^{3}/$_4$	cup roasted, lightly salted shelled sunflower seeds
1	cup quick-cooking oats, uncooked
7	cups crisp rice cereal
1	cup honey
1	cup sugar
1^1/$_2$	cups crunchy-style peanut butter
1	cup powdered milk
1	teaspoon vanilla extract
^{1}/$_2$	teaspoon almond extract

◆ Lightly spray a 15x10x1-inch jelly roll pan with nonstick cooking spray; set aside.

◆ Combine the dried cranberries, carob chips, and sunflower seeds in a food processor. Pulse to chop until coarsely chopped (about 3–4 pulses). Transfer to a large bowl and mix in the oats and crisp rice cereal.

◆ In a medium saucepan mix the honey, sugar, and peanut butter. Cook and stir over low heat until blended and bubbly. Remove from heat and stir in the powdered milk, vanilla, and almond extract. Pour the peanut butter mixture over the cereal mixture; mix with a wooden spoon until evenly coated.

◆ With a large square of wax paper, press the mixture into the prepared pan. Cool 15 minutes. Cut into 24 bars. Cool completely before removing from the pan. Store in covered containers between layers of wax paper. ◆ Makes 24 big bars.

Cereal Bars

Caramel Apple Bars

So easy and so good, these really do taste like caramel apples thanks to the apple juice concentrate and dried apples.

8	cups sweetened puffed wheat cereal
1$^1/_2$	cups chopped dried apples
$^1/_2$	cup chopped roasted almonds or peanuts
1	14-ounce package caramels, unwrapped
$^1/_2$	of a 6-ounce container frozen apple juice concentrate, thawed

◆ Lightly spray a 13x9x2-inch baking pan with nonstick cooking spray; set aside.

◆ In a large bowl mix the cereal, dried apples, and nuts.

◆ In a medium microwavable bowl microwave the caramels and apple juice concentrate on high for 2 minutes or until caramels are melted, stirring every minute. Immediately pour over cereal mixture; mix lightly until well coated.

◆ With a large square of wax paper, press into the prepared pan. Refrigerate 30 minutes or until firm. Cut into 24 bars. Store in covered containers between layers of wax paper. ◆ Makes 24 bars.

Variation:
Caramel Nut Bars: Replace the dried apples and $^1/_2$ cup almonds with 1$^1/_2$ cups lightly salted roasted nuts, any variety, coarsely chopped. Use 3 tablespoons milk in place of the juice concentrate.

Cereal Bars

Pineapple Macadamia Bars

Whip up a batch of these bars for a mouth-watering tropical escape.

7¹/₃	cups sweetened puffed wheat cereal
1	cup roasted, coarsely chopped, salted macadamia nuts
1	cup coarsely chopped dried pineapple
1	14-ounce package caramels
2	tablespoons fresh lime juice
2	teaspoons grated lime zest
1	teaspoon ground ginger

◈ Lightly spray a 13x9x2-inch baking pan with nonstick cooking spray; set aside.

◈ In a large bowl mix the cereal, macadamia nuts, and pineapple.

◈ Microwave caramels and lime juice in medium microwavable bowl on high 2 minutes or until caramels are melted, stirring every minute; stir in lime zest and ground ginger. Immediately pour over cereal mixture; mix lightly until well coated.

◈ With a large square of wax paper, press into the prepared pan. Refrigerate until firm. Cut into 24 bars. Store in covered containers between layers of wax paper. ◈ Makes 24 big bars.

Cereal Bars

PINEAPPLE MACADAMIA BARS

Cookie Bars

No-Bake Brownies

The simplicity of chocolate brownies is one of life's greatest (eating) pleasures. Here the well-loved confection takes shape in a quick and easy no-bake bar. You can doctor this brownie recipe to suit your taste in the same way you would regular brownies. For example, replace the vanilla with a different extract (e.g., peppermint, brandy, rum, orange, maple), use any nut of your choice, spice it up with cinnamon or a dash of red pepper, or a add a favorite purchased or homemade frosting.

2¹/₂	cups finely crushed chocolate graham cracker crumbs
2	cups miniature marshmallows
1	cup chopped walnuts or pecans, preferably skillet toasted and cooled (see page 8)
1	cup semisweet chocolate chips
1	cup canned evaporated milk
¹/₂	cup light corn syrup
¹/₄	teaspoon salt
1	tablespoon butter
1	tablespoon vanilla extract

◆ Lightly spray a 9x9x2-inch baking pan with nonstick cooking spray; set aside.

◆ In a large bowl mix the crumbs, marshmallows, and nuts; set aside.

◆ In a medium saucepan combine the chocolate chips, evaporated milk, corn syrup, and salt. Stir over low heat until chocolate is melted. Increase heat to medium; heat to a full boil. Boil for 10 minutes, stirring constantly. Remove from heat and stir in butter and vanilla until blended.

◆ Immediately stir chocolate mixture into the crumb mixture, mixing until well blended. Spread evenly in prepared pan, pressing down and smoothing surface with a square of wax paper. Refrigerate until set, about 3 hours. Cut into 24 bars. Store in covered containers between layers of wax paper. ◆ Makes 24 bars.

Cookie Bars
NO-BAKE BROWNIES

Cashew Blondies

Butterscotch lovers will love this no-bake rendition of classic blondies. Although scrumptious with cashews, you can substitute the roasted nut of your choice, from almonds to macadamias to peanuts.

$2^1/_2$	cups finely crushed graham cracker crumbs
2	cups miniature marshmallows
1	cup lightly salted roasted cashews, chopped
1	cup butterscotch baking chips
1	cup canned evaporated milk
$^1/_2$	cup light corn syrup
1	tablespoon butter
1	tablespoon vanilla extract

◆ Lightly spray a 9x9x2-inch baking pan with nonstick cooking spray; set aside.

◆ In a large bowl mix the crumbs, marshmallows, and cashews; set aside.

◆ In a medium saucepan combine the butterscotch chips, evaporated milk, and corn syrup. Stir over low heat until butterscotch chips are melted. Increase heat to medium; heat to a full boil. Boil for 10 minutes, stirring constantly. Remove from heat and stir in butter and vanilla until blended.

◆ Immediately stir butterscotch mixture into the crumb mixture, mixing until well blended. Spread evenly in prepared pan, pressing down and smoothing surface with a square of wax paper. Refrigerate until set, about 3 hours. Cut into 24 bars. Store in covered containers between layers of wax paper. ◆ Makes 24 bars.

Cookie Bars

CASHEW BLONDIES

Lemon Cookie Squares

Brew a cup of Earl Grey when it's chilly or pour a glass of iced tea when it's sizzling—either way, these creamy-crunchy lemon cookies will fit the bill.

1¹/₃	cups white chocolate chips
¹/₂	cup (1 stick) butter
2	teaspoons grated lemon zest
1¹/₃	cups coursely crushed lemon creme sandwich cookies
1	cup chopped pecans, preferably skillet toasted and cooled (see page 8)

◆ Line an 8x8x2-inch pan with foil (see page 12); lightly spray with nonstick cooking spray. Set aside.

◆ Place the white chocolate chips and butter in a medium saucepan set over low heat. Cook and stir until the white chocolate is completely melted.

◆ Remove from heat; stir in zest, cookies, and pecans, mixing well. Quickly spread mixture into prepared pan.

◆ Refrigerate bars 3 hours or until firm. Cut into 16 squares. Store in covered containers between layers of wax paper. ◆ Makes 16 squares.

Cookie Bars
LEMON COOKIE SQUARES

Black-Bottomed Butterscotch Bars

These showy cookies feature a rich, dark chocolate bottom, a smooth butter-scotch top and a crunchy crown of peanuts. They'll surely attract a following of enthusiasts whenever you make them.

6	tablespoons ($^3/_4$ stick) butter, melted
1	cup creamy peanut butter
1$^1/_2$	cups sifted powdered sugar
1	9-ounce package chocolate wafers, crushed into crumbs
1	11-ounce package (about 2 cups) butterscotch baking chips
$^1/_4$	cup heavy whipping cream
$^3/_4$	cup chopped roasted, lightly salted peanuts or cashews

◆ Set aside an ungreased 13x9x2-inch baking pan.

◆ In a large mixing bowl mix the melted butter, peanut butter, and powdered sugar with a wooden spoon until blended. Stir in the chocolate wafer crumbs until combined. Press evenly into prepared pan, pressing down and smoothing surface with a square of wax paper. Refrigerate while preparing topping.

◆ In a heavy medium saucepan set over low heat melt the butterscotch chips with the whipping cream, stirring until melted and smooth.

◆ Spoon and spread butterscotch mixture over crumb mixture; sprinkle with the nuts. Refrigerate until set, about 2 hours. Cut into 48 bars. Store in covered containers between layers of wax paper. ◆ Makes 48 bars.

Cookie Bars

No-Bake Hello Dollies

Ideal for backyard barbecues, this no-bake rendition of the favorite multi-layered bar will garner high praise—and requests for the recipe.

1	cup (2 sticks) butter, divided use
2$^1/_2$	cups finely crushed graham cracker crumbs
$^1/_2$	cup plus 2 tablespoons firmly packed light brown sugar, divided use
$^1/_3$	cup canned evaporated milk
2$^1/_4$	cups miniature marshmallows
1	cup butterscotch baking chips
1	cup chopped walnuts or pecans, preferably skillet toasted and cooled (see page 8)
1$^1/_3$	cups shredded coconut, skillet toasted and cooled (see page 8)
1	cup miniature semisweet chocolate chips

◆ Line a 13x9x2-inch pan with foil (see page 12); lightly spray with nonstick cooking spray. Set aside.

◆ In a large nonstick skillet set over medium-low heat melt $^3/_4$ cup of the butter. In a large bowl mix the graham cracker crumbs and 2 tablespoons brown sugar with the melted butter until blended. Transfer crumb mixture to prepared pan, pressing down and smoothing surface with a square of wax paper. Refrigerate while preparing topping.

◆ In a large saucepan place the remaining $^1/_2$ cup brown sugar, evaporated milk, marshmallows, and remaining $^1/_4$ cup butter; cook on medium heat until mixture comes to a boil, stirring constantly. Boil 5 minutes, stirring constantly. Add butterscotch chips; cook until completely melted, stirring frequently.

◆ Pour and spread mixture over prepared crust to cover evenly. Immediately sprinkle with nuts, coconut, and miniature chocolate chips; press lightly into chocolate layer. Refrigerate until set, about 3 hours. Cut into 36 bars. Store in covered containers between layers of wax paper. ◆ Makes 36 bars.

Cookie Bars

Chocolate Caramel Peanut Bars

You'll savor every bite of these caramel and chocolate-rich bars.

1 1/2   **cups roasted peanuts, divided use**
1   **sleeve saltine crackers (about 38 crackers), coarsely broken**
1   **cup semisweet miniature chocolate chips**
1   **cup miniature marshmallows**
1/2   **cup (1 stick) butter**
1   **14-ounce package caramels (about 50), unwrapped**

◆ Lightly spray a 13x9x2-inch pan with nonstick cooking spray; set aside.

◆ Chop 1/2 cup of the peanuts; set aside. In large bowl mix remaining 1 cup peanuts, the cracker pieces, miniature chocolate chips, and marshmallows; set aside.

◆ Place the butter and caramels in a medium saucepan; cook on low heat until caramels are completely melted and mixture is well blended, stirring frequently. Pour over cracker mixture, tossing to coat well.

◆ Gently press cracker mixture firmly into prepared pan with a square of wax paper. Sprinkle with reserved chopped peanuts; press gently into bars with square of wax paper. Refrigerate 30 minutes or until completely cooled. Cut into 36 bars. Store in covered containers between layers of wax paper. ◆ Makes 36 bars.

Cookie Bars

Cinnamon Bars
with Cream Cheese Frosting

The down-home flavor of these cream cheese-frosted, cinnamon-y bars will surely bring back memories of cookies past.

2	large eggs, lightly beaten
1	cup firmly packed dark brown sugar
$^3/_4$	cup (1$^1/_2$ sticks) butter
2	teaspoons ground cinnamon
2$^1/_2$	cups gingersnap crumbs
2	cups miniature marshmallows
$^1/_2$	cup finely chopped pecans, preferably skillet-toasted and cooled
1	8-ounce package cream cheese, softened
1	teaspoon vanilla extract
2	cups powdered sugar
3/4	tablespoons milk

◆ Lightly spray a 9x9x2-inch pan with nonstick cooking spray; set aside.

◆ In a large saucepan combine the beaten eggs, brown sugar, butter, and cinnamon. Bring to a boil and let cook on low for 2 minutes, stirring constantly. Remove from heat. Add the gingersnap crumbs, marshmallows, and pecans, mixing until blended. Transfer mixture to prepared pan, pressing down and smoothing surface with a square of wax paper. Cool completely. Refrigerate while preparing topping.

◆ Using an electric mixer, beat the cream cheese in a medium bowl until smooth. Add vanilla and powdered sugar and beat until smooth. Beat in enough of the milk to make frosting of spreading consistency. Spread frosting over bars. Refrigerate overnight. Cut into 24 small bars. Store in covered containers between layers of wax paper. ◆ Makes 24 bars.

Cookie Bars

Tri-Level Caramel Bars

These showstopper bars will dazzle your friends. They'll be even more amazed that no baking is required to turn out these triple-decker treats.

1	cup (2 sticks) butter, melted, divided use
4	cups powdered sugar
1^1/$_2$	cups graham cracker crumbs
1^1/$_2$	cups peanut butter
1^1/$_2$	cups coarsely chopped roasted cashews or peanuts, divided use
1	14-ounce package caramels (about 50 pieces), unwrapped
^{1}/$_4$	cup milk
1^1/$_3$	cups milk or semisweet chocolate chips

❖ Lightly spray a 13x9x2-inch pan with nonstick cooking spray; set aside.

❖ In a small saucepan melt ^{3}/$_4$ cup (1^1/$_2$ sticks) butter. In a large bowl mix the melted butter, powdered sugar, graham cracker crumbs, peanut butter, and 1 cup of the chopped nuts. Transfer mixture to prepared pan, pressing down and smoothing surface with a square of wax paper. Refrigerate while preparing topping.

❖ In a large saucepan set over low heat melt the caramels and milk, stirring frequently until mixture is melted and smooth. Pour over crust.

❖ Melt chocolate with remaining ^{1}/$_4$ cup butter in large saucepan on low heat, stirring frequently until melted and smooth. Spread over caramel layer. Immediately sprinkle with remaining nuts. Refrigerate at least 1 hour. Cut into 36 bars. Store in covered containers between layers of wax paper. ❖ Makes 36 small bars.

Cookie Bars

TRI-LEVEL CARAMEL BARS

Milk Chocolate Orange Bars

The flavors of chocolate and orange are very good together. These bars are very tasty, very rich, and very much worth every bite.

3	cups finely crushed chocolate graham cracker crumbs
1¹/₂	cups miniature marshmallows
1	cup chopped almonds
²/₃	cup firmly packed light brown sugar
1	cup canned evaporated milk
2	cups milk chocolate chips
1	tablespoon grated orange zest
¹/₂	teaspoon almond extract

◆ Lightly spray a 9x9x2-inch pan with nonstick cooking spray; set aside.

◆ In a large bowl combine the chocolate graham cracker crumbs, marshmallows, almonds, and brown sugar.

◆ In a medium saucepan set over low heat combine the evaporated milk and milk chocolate chips. Cook and stir until chips are melted and mixture is smooth. Mix in orange zest and almond extract. Pour all but ¹/₂ cup of the melted chocolate over crumb mixture; toss and stir to coat evenly.

◆ Immediately spread mixture into prepared pan. Press and smooth surface with a square of wax paper. Drizzle reserved chocolate mixture over bars. Refrigerate 2–3 hours or as long as overnight. Cut into 24 bars. Store in covered containers between layers of wax paper. ◆ Makes 24 bars.

Cookie Bars

MILK CHOCOLATE ORANGE BARS

Tart Cherry Caramel Bars

The tart dried cherries in these bars are the perfect counterpoint to the velvety caramel and crunchy almonds.

1¹⁄₂	**sleeves (approximately 57 crackers) coarsely broken saltine crackers**
2	**cups white chocolate chips**
1	**cup miniature marshmallows**
³⁄₄	**cup tart dried cherries or dried cranberries**
1	**cup chopped roasted, lightly salted almonds, divided use**
¹⁄₂	**cup (1 stick) butter**
1	**14-ounce package caramels (about 50), unwrapped**
³⁄₄	**teaspoon almond extract**

◆ Lightly spray a 13x9x2-inch pan with nonstick cooking spray; set aside.

◆ In large bowl mix the crushed crackers, white chocolate chips, marshmallows, cherries, and half of the chopped almonds; set aside.

◆ Place the butter and caramels in small saucepan. Cook and stir over low heat until caramels are completely melted and mixture is well blended, stirring frequently. Stir in almond extract. Pour over cracker mixture; toss to coat well.

◆ Working quickly, press the mixture into the prepared pan, pressing down with a square of wax paper; sprinkle with reserved chopped almonds. Refrigerate 30 minutes or until completely cooled. Cut into 24 bars. Store in covered containers between layers of wax paper. ◆ Makes 24 big bars.

Cookie Bars

TART CHERRY CARAMEL BARS

Rum Raisin Bars

This is definitely an adult cookie. Perfumed with nutmeg and orange zest, they are excellent additions to holiday cookie plates.

2	**tablespoons butter**
3	**cups miniature marshmallows**
2	**teaspoons grated orange zest**
2	**teaspoons rum-flavored extract**
¹/₄	**teaspoon ground nutmeg**
1	**cup finely crushed crisp sugar cookies**
³/₄	**cup golden raisins**
¹/₂	**cup chopped walnuts, skillet toasted and cooled (see page 8)**

❖ Lightly spray an 8x8x2-inch pan with nonstick cooking spray; set aside.

❖ In a large saucepan set over low heat melt the butter. Add the marshmallows, stirring constantly, until marshmallows are melted. Remove from heat; stir in the orange zest, rum extract, and nutmeg.

❖ Stir in the cookie crumbs, raisins, and walnuts; mix until well blended. Transfer mixture to prepared pan, pressing down and smoothing surface with a square of wax paper. Refrigerate at least 1 hour. Cut into 16 small bars. Store in covered containers between layers of wax paper. ❖ Makes 16 bars.

Cookie Bars

Dulce de Leche Truffle Bars

Offer these sophisticated bars with strong cups of coffee or espresso drinks for a grown-up, coffeehouse-style splurge.

1	cup (2 sticks) butter, melted, divided use
2$^1/_2$	cups finely crushed crisp shortbread cookie crumbs
1	cup firmly packed dark brown sugar
1	5-ounce can evaporated milk (about $^2/_3$ cup)
1	10-ounce package miniature marshmallows
2	cups butterscotch baking chips
2	teaspoons vanilla extract
1	cup toffee baking bits, divided use

◆ Foil-line a 13x9x2-inch baking pan (see page 12); set aside.

◆ In a large skillet melt $^3/_4$ cup (1$^1/_2$ sticks) of the butter over medium heat. In a large bowl mix the melted butter with the cookie crumbs. Transfer mixture to prepared pan, pressing down and smoothing surface with a square of wax paper. Refrigerate while preparing topping.

◆ In a large saucepan place the brown sugar, evaporated milk, marshmallows, and remaining $^1/_4$ cup butter. Cook over medium-high heat, stirring constantly, until mixture comes to boil. Boil 5 minutes, stirring constantly. Reduce heat to medium-low and add the butterscotch chips. Stir until chips are completely melted. Remove from heat; stir in the vanilla extract and $^1/_2$ cup of the toffee bits.

◆ Pour mixture over prepared crust; spread evenly to cover. Sprinkle with the remaining toffee bits. Refrigerate 2 hours or until firm. Cut into 36 small bars. Store in covered containers between layers of wax paper. ◆ Makes 36 bars.

Cookie Bars

Peanut Butter Cup Bars

Here's a great everyday cookie, loaded with the favorite flavors of chocolate and peanut butter, quick to make, and sturdy enough for weekday lunch bags.

$^3/_4$	cup (1$^1/_2$ sticks) butter, softened
2	cups peanut butter, divided use
1	teaspoon vanilla extract
2	cups powdered sugar, divided use
3	cups graham cracker crumbs
2	cups miniature semisweet chocolate chips, divided use

◆ Lightly spray a 13x9x2-inch pan with nonstick cooking spray; set aside.

◆ In a large bowl beat the butter, 1$^1/_4$ cups peanut butter, and vanilla with an electric mixer on medium-high speed until well blended and creamy.

◆ Turn mixer speed to low; gradually beat in 1 cup of the powdered sugar. Using a wooden spoon, mix in remaining powdered sugar, graham cracker crumbs, and $^1/_2$ cup of the chocolate chips. Using a large square of wax paper, press the mixture firmly and evenly into prepared pan.

◆ In a medium saucepan melt the remaining $^3/_4$ cup peanut butter and 1$^1/_2$ cups chocolate chips over lowest possible heat, stirring constantly, until smooth. Spread mixture over graham cracker crust in pan. Chill for at least 1 hour or until chocolate is firm. Cut into 24 bars. Store in covered containers between layers of wax paper. ◆ Makes 24 big bars.

Cookie Bars

Raspberry Linzer Bars

Reminiscent of the classic Austrian torte of the same name, these bars are elegant enough to serve as a finale to a first-rate supper.

$3/4$	cup (1$1/2$ sticks) butter, softened
1$1/4$	cups almond butter
1	teaspoon almond extract
2	cups powdered sugar, divided use
3	cups graham cracker crumbs
$2/3$	cup seedless raspberry preserves, stirred to loosen
1	cup white chocolate chips
2	teaspoons vegetable shortening

◈ Lightly spray a 9x9x2-inch pan with nonstick cooking spray; set aside.

◈ In a large bowl beat the butter, almond butter, and almond extract with an electric mixer set on medium-high speed until well blended and creamy.

◈ Turn mixer speed to low; gradually beat in 1 cup of the powdered sugar. Using a wooden spoon, mix in graham cracker crumbs and remaining 1 cup powdered sugar. Reserve 1 cup of the mixture. Using a large square of wax paper, press the remaining mixture firmly and evenly into prepared pan.

◈ Spread bars with raspberry jam. Sprinkle with reserved crumb mixture, using fingertips to gently press into jam layer.

◈ In a small saucepan melt the white chocolate chips and shortening over the lowest possible heat, stirring constantly, until smooth. Drizzle mixture over bars. Chill for at least 1 hour or until chocolate is firm; cut into 24 bars. Store in covered containers between layers of wax paper. ◈ Makes 24 small bars.

Cookie Bars

Variation:

Sacher Torte Bars: Prepare as directed above but use chocolate graham crackers in place of regular graham crackers, apricot jam or preserves in place of the raspberry preserves, and semisweet chocolate chips in place of the white chocolate chips.

Panforte Bars

These bars are based on the Italian fruitcake known as panforte, a dense cake rich with candied fruit, spices, cocoa, and nuts. The bars make a great ending to a holiday dinner.

2	cups finely ground vanilla wafers (about 44 wafers)
3/4	cup powdered sugar
2	tablespoons unsweetened cocoa powder
1	teaspoon pumpkin pie spice
1/2	cup (1 stick) butter, melted
1/4	cup brandy
1	cup chopped mixed candied fruit and peels
1/2	cup chopped dried apricots
1/2	cup chopped dates
	Powdered sugar to coat

◆ Line a 9x9x2-inch square pan with foil (see page 12). Lightly coat foil with nonstick cooking spray.

◆ In a large bowl combine the ground wafers, powdered sugar, cocoa powder, and pumpkin pie spice. Add the melted butter and brandy; stir to combine and coat well. Add the candied fruit, dried apricots, and dates; mix well to combine.

◆ Turn mixture into prepared pan. Using a square of wax paper or moist fingers, press into prepared pan (mixture will seem slightly wet and sticky; it will set up as it chills). Loosely cover and refrigerate overnight.

◆ Cut bars into 24 pieces. Liberally dust with powdered sugar to coat. Store in covered containers between layers of wax paper. ◆ Makes 24 bars.

Cookie Bars

Apple Scotchies

Two harmonious flavors—apple and butterscotch—are united in these vanilla cream-frosted bars. Apple cider is the perfect accompaniment.

9	tablespoons butter, softened, divided use
1	cup butterscotch baking chips, divided use
$^1/_3$	cup firmly packed light brown sugar
2	cups graham cracker crumbs
1	cup very finely chopped dried apples
$^1/_2$	cup finely chopped pecans
2	cups powdered sugar, sifted
1	3-ounce package cream cheese, softened
$2^1/_2$	tablespoons milk
1	teaspoon vanilla extract

◇ Lightly spray a 9x9x2-inch pan with nonstick cooking spray; set aside.

◇ In a medium saucepan melt 8 tablespoons (1 stick) of the butter with $^1/_2$ cup of the butterscotch chips. Remove from the heat and stir in the brown sugar, graham cracker crumbs, dried apples, and pecans. Press mixture into prepared pan with a large square of wax paper. Chill for 1 hour.

◇ In a medium bowl blend the powdered sugar, cream cheese, milk, and vanilla with an electric mixer set on medium speed until mixture has an icing-like consistency; spread over the chilled bars. Chill for 30 minutes.

◇ Melt the remaining 1 tablespoon butter with the remaining $^1/_2$ cup butterscotch chips, stirring until mixture is smooth. Spread or drizzle over the top of the bars. Chill for 1–2 hours. Cut into 16 squares by dipping a sharp knife in hot water and let it melt through the butterscotch. Store in covered containers between layers of wax paper. ◇ Makes 16 squares.

Cookie Bars
APPLE SCOTCHIES

Nanaimo Bars

They may not be well-known in the States (yet!), but Nanaimo bars are Canadian cookie classics. Although they are named after the town of Nanaimo in British Columbia, no one is quite sure why or how or when the recipe originated. What is certain is they are scrumptious bars, suitable for any time of the year and any occasion.

$^1/_4$	cup sugar
5	tablespoons unsweetened cocoa powder
1	cup plus 2 tablespoons ($2^1/_4$ sticks) butter, softened, divided use
1	large egg, beaten
$1^1/_4$	cups graham cracker crumbs
$^1/_2$	cup finely chopped pecans, walnuts, or almonds
1	cup sweetened flake coconut
$2^1/_2$	tablespoons milk
2	tablespoons vanilla instant pudding and pie filling powder (from a 4-serving-size package)
2	cups powdered sugar
4	1-ounce squares semisweet baking chocolate

◆ Lightly spray an 8x8x2-inch pan with nonstick cooking spray; set aside.

◆ In the top of a double boiler set over simmering water combine the sugar, cocoa, and $^1/_2$ cup (1 stick) butter. Cook and stir until melted and blended. Add the beaten egg; cook and stir 1 minute. Remove from heat. Stir in the graham cracker crumbs, nuts, and coconut. Press firmly into prepared pan with a large square of wax paper. Refrigerate for 1 hour.

◆ In a medium bowl beat the milk, pudding powder, powdered sugar, and $^1/_2$ cup (1 stick) of the remaining butter with an electric mixer set on low speed,

Cookie Bars

beating until light and well blended. Spread over chilled base. Refrigerate for 30 minutes.

◇ In a small saucepan melt the chocolate with the remaining 2 tablespoons butter over low heat. Remove from heat; cool 5 minutes. Pour and spread over bars. Refrigerate for 30 minutes. Cut into 16 bars. Store in covered container, in the refrigerator, between layers of wax paper. ◇ Makes 16 bars.

Variations:

Kahlua Nanaimo Bars: Prepare as directed above but substitute $2^1/_2$ tablespoons Kahlua or other coffee liqueur for the milk.

Chocolate Peppermint Nanaimo Bars: Prepare as directed above but add 1 teaspoon peppermint extract and 1–2 drops of red food coloring, if desired, to the pudding layer. Sprinkle the third (chocolate) layer with $^1/_2$ cup coarsely crushed red & white-striped peppermint candies or candy canes.

Pistachio Nanaimo Bars: Prepare as directed above but substitute 2 tablespoons pistachio instant pudding powder for the vanilla powder. Sprinkle the third (chocolate) layer with $^1/_2$ cup coarsely chopped pistachio nuts.

Cookie Bars
NANAIMO BARS

Cappuccino Bars

If you love coffee or espresso drinks, you'll savor the flavor of these rich, layered bars.

9	tablespoons butter, softened, divided use
6	1-ounce squares semisweet chocolate, divided use
$^1/_3$	cup firmly packed light brown sugar
2	cups chocolate wafer or chocolate graham cracker crumbs
1	cup finely chopped walnuts
1	teaspoon vanilla extract
2	teaspoons instant espresso or coffee powder
2	cups powdered sugar, sifted
1	3-ounce package cream cheese, softened
$2^1/_2$	tablespoons milk

◆ Lightly spray an 9x9x2-inch pan with nonstick cooking spray; set aside.

◆ In a medium saucepan melt 8 tablespoons (1 stick) of the butter with 3 squares of the chocolate. Remove from the heat; stir in the brown sugar, chocolate wafer crumbs, and walnuts. Press mixture into prepared pan with a large square of wax paper. Chill for 1 hour.

◆ In a small cup combine the vanilla and espresso powder, stirring until dissolved. In a medium bowl blend the espresso mixture, powdered sugar, cream cheese, and milk with an electric mixer set on medium until mixture has an icing-like consistency; spread over bars. Chill for 30 minutes.

◆ Melt the remaining 1 tablespoon butter with the remaining 3 squares of chocolate, stirring until mixture is smooth. Spread over the top of the bars. Chill for 1–2 hours. Cut into 16 squares by dipping a sharp knife in hot water and let it melt through the chocolate. Store in covered containers between layers of wax paper. ◆ Makes 16 squares.

Cookie Bars

Cranberry Orange Bars

Super-saturated with flavor, these easy bars are both cozy in winter and cool in summer.

2	tablespoons ($^1/_4$ stick) butter
3	cups miniature marshmallows
$2^1/_2$	cups coarsely crushed crisp sugar cookies
$^3/_4$	cup dried cranberries
1	tablespoon grated orange zest
$^1/_2$	cup coarsely chopped honey-roasted almonds

◆ Lightly spray an 8x8x2-inch pan with nonstick cooking spray; set aside.

◆ In a large saucepan set over low heat, melt the butter. Add the marshmallows; cook and stir until marshmallows are melted and mixture is smooth. Remove from heat. Stir in the cookie crumbs, cranberries, orange zest, and almonds; spread into prepared pan with a large square of wax paper.

◆ Refrigerate 1 hour or until firm. Cut into 16 bars. Store in covered containers between layers of wax paper. ◆ Makes 16 bars.

Cookie Bars

Cookies & Cream Bars

Semisweet chocolate and vanilla pudding mix transform chocolate sandwich cookies into sublime treats.

28	creme-filled chocolate sandwich cookies
$^1/_4$	cup ($^1/_2$ stick) butter
$^1/_3$	cup milk
1	4-serving-size package vanilla instant pudding & pie filling
1	cup powdered sugar
1	teaspoon vanilla extract
2	1-ounce squares semisweet baking chocolate, coarsely chopped

❖ Lightly spray a 9x9x2-inch pan with nonstick cooking spray; set aside.

❖ Finely crush 20 of the cookies; set aside. Coarsely crush the remaining 8 cookies; set aside.

❖ In large microwavable bowl microwave the butter on high for 30 seconds or until butter is melted. Add the 20 finely crushed cookies; mix well. With a large square of wax paper, press crumb mixture firmly onto bottom of prepared pan.

❖ In a small microwavable bowl microwave the milk on high 1 minute or until very hot. Whisk in dry pudding mix, powdered sugar, and vanilla until well blended. Pour over crust; spread to completely cover crust. Sprinkle with reserved coarsely crushed cookies.

❖ Place the chopped chocolate squares in small microwavable bowl. Microwave on high 45 seconds; stir until chocolate is completely melted. Drizzle melted chocolate over pudding mixture. Refrigerate 1 hour or until set. Cut into 20 bars. Store in covered containers between layers of wax paper. ❖ Makes 20 bars.

Cookie Bars

COOKIES & CREAM BARS

Chocolate Hazelnut Fudge Bars

Chocolate and hazelnut pair perfectly, as these streamlined treats deliciously demonstrate.

18	double chocolate fudge sandwich cookies, divided use
6	squares semisweet baking chocolate squares, divided use
5	tablespoons butter, divided use
1	4-serving-size package instant chocolate pudding & pie filling
1 1/2	cups powdered sugar
1/3	cup boiling water
1/2	cup chocolate-hazelnut spread (e.g., Nutella®)

◆ Lightly spray an 8x8x2-inch pan with nonstick cooking spray; set aside.

◆ Finely crush 12 of the cookies; set aside. Coarsely crush remaining 6 cookies; set aside.

◆ In a medium saucepan melt 3 of the chocolate squares and 4 tablespoons (1/2 stick) butter over low heat, stirring until completely melted. Stir until chocolate is completely melted and mixture is well blended. Stir in the finely crushed cookies. With a large square of wax paper, firmly press into prepared pan.

◆ In a medium bowl combine dry pudding mix and powdered sugar. Gradually add the boiling water, stirring until well blended. Whisk in the chocolate-hazelnut spread until well blended. Spread evenly to cover bottom of crust.

◆ In a small saucepan melt the remaining chocolate squares and 1 tablespoon butter; stir until chocolate is completely melted. Carefully spread over the pudding mixture; sprinkle the coarsely crushed cookies over bars. Refrigerate at least 1 hour or until set. Cut into 16 bars. Store in covered containers between layers of wax paper. ◆ Makes 16 bars.

Banana Crunch Bars

These make a great ending to a warm-weather gathering. And because bananas are available year-round, you can enjoy them no matter what the season. Be sure to select bananas that are ripe, but still firm, for best results.

$^1/_2$	cup plus 2 tablespoons (1$^1/_4$ sticks) butter, softened, divided use
$^1/_4$	cup packed brown sugar
2	cups chocolate wafer or chocolate graham cracker crumbs
3	tablespoons light corn syrup
2	medium firm bananas, peeked and diced (about 1$^1/_2$ cups)
1	teaspoon rum-flavored extract
1	cup milk or semisweet chocolate chips
1	teaspoon vegetable shortening

◆ Set aside an ungreased 8x8x2-inch baking pan.

◆ In a small saucepan set over low heat melt $^1/_2$ cup (1 stick) of the butter. In a medium mixing bowl combine the melted butter, brown sugar, and chocolate wafer crumbs with fingers or a wooden spoon until well blended. With a large square of wax paper, press mixture into the bottom of prepared pan. Chill about 20 minutes or until firm.

◆ In a small saucepan combine the corn syrup and remaining 2 tablespoons butter. Stir over medium heat until melted and bubbly. Remove from heat; stir in bananas and rum extract. Spoon banana mixture in an even layer over prepared crust.

◆ In a small saucepan melt the chocolate chips and shortening over low heat, stirring until melted and smooth; drizzle over the banana layer. Cover and chill until set. Cut into 16 bars. Store, loosely covered with plastic wrap, in the refrigerator. ◆ Makes 16 bars.

Cookie Bars

Caramel Fudge Bars

With a dream-team combination of caramel and chocolate fudge, these bars could win any popularity contest.

54	flaky, buttery rectangular crackers (e.g., Waverly® or Club® crackers)
1	14-ounce can sweetened condensed milk
1	cup firmly packed dark brown sugar
$^1/_2$	cup (1 stick) butter
6	tablespoons milk, divided use
1	cup graham cracker crumbs
1	cup semisweet chocolate chips
1	cup creamy peanut butter

◆ Lightly spray a 13x9x2-inch pan with nonstick cooking spray; set aside. Place half of the crackers in bottom of the prepared pan.

◆ In a medium saucepan combine the sweetened condensed milk, brown sugar, butter, and 4 tablespoons ($^1/_4$ cup) of the milk. Cook over low heat until butter is melted, stirring frequently. Increase heat to medium-high; bring to a boil. Boil 5 minutes, stirring constantly. Remove from heat and stir in the graham cracker crumbs.

◆ Pour and spread half of caramel mixture over crackers in pan. Arrange remaining crackers over caramel. Top with remaining caramel mixture.

◆ In a small saucepan heat the chocolate chips and remaining 2 tablespoons milk over low heat, stirring until chocolate is melted and smooth. Stir in the peanut butter until well blended. Spread chocolate mixture over bars. Refrigerate 30 minutes or until set. Cut into 36 bars. Store in covered containers between layers of wax paper. ◆ Makes 36 bars.

Cookie Bars
CARAMEL FUDGE BARS

Chocolate Raspberry Truffle Bars

A combination of rich and richer, these confections are a scrumptious mix of two favorite flavors: chocolate and raspberry. For an extra-special treat, poke 24 fresh raspberries into the chocolate mixture before chilling, then cut into squares with a raspberry in the center of each square.

$1/2$	cup plus 1 tablespoon butter, divided use
$1/4$	cup packed light brown sugar
2	cups chocolate wafer or chocolate graham cracker crumbs
$1/3$	cup canned sweetened condensed milk
3	tablespoons seedless raspberry jam
$1\,1/3$	cups semisweet chocolate chips
1–2	tablespoons powdered sugar

◆ Foil-line an 8x8x2-inch baking pan (see page 12); set aside.

◆ Melt $1/2$ cup (1 stick) of the butter. In a medium mixing bowl combine the melted butter, brown sugar, and chocolate wafer crumbs with a wooden spoon until well blended. With a large square of wax paper, press mixture into bottom of prepared pan; chill about 20 minutes or until firm.

◆ In a medium saucepan combine the condensed milk, jam, and remaining tablespoon butter. Cook and stir over low heat until mixture is melted and smooth, about 2–3 minutes. Stir in chocolate chips; cook and stir until melted and smooth. Pour mixture over prepared crust. Cover and chill 2 hours until set. Cut into 24 bars and sprinkle with powdered sugar. Store in covered containers between layers of wax paper. ◆ Makes 24 small bars.

Cookie Bars

Toasted Coconut Fudge Bars

These chocolate confections rest on the cusp of cookie and candy. They have a deep chocolate, truffle-like flavor accented by the slightly nutty flavor of toasted coconut. If you have the time and inclination, you can skillet-toast the walnuts, too, to deepen their flavor.

1	cup (2 sticks) butter, divided use
2$^1/_2$	cups finely crushed graham cracker crumbs
1	cup sugar
1	5-ounce can evaporated milk (about $^2/_3$ cup)
1	10-ounce package miniature marshmallows
2	cups semisweet chocolate chips
1	cup chopped walnuts
1	cup shredded coconut, skillet toasted (see page 8)

❖ Foil-line a 13x9x2-inch baking pan (see page 12); set aside.

❖ In a small saucepan melt $^3/_4$ cup (1$^1/_2$ sticks) of the butter. In a medium bowl mix the melted butter and graham cracker crumbs until blended. With a large square of wax paper, press into bottom of prepared pan. Chill while preparing topping.

❖ In a large saucepan place the sugar, evaporated milk, marshmallows, and remaining $^1/_4$ cup ($^1/_2$ stick) butter. Cook and stir over medium heat until mixture comes to boil, stirring constantly. Boil 5 minutes, stirring constantly. Remove from heat and add the chocolate chips, stirring until chips are completely melted.

❖ Pour the chocolate mixture over the crust, spreading evenly to cover. Sprinkle with the walnuts and coconut; press lightly into chocolate layer. Refrigerate 2 hours or until firm. Cut into 36 bars. Store in covered containers between layers of wax paper. ❖ Makes 36 bars.

Cookie Bars

Toasted Almond-Apricot Truffle Bars

Almonds add crunch, while apricots give these very rich cookies some chewiness. You can vary the bars in any number of ways. For example, vary the type of dried fruit, use lemon or lime zest in place of orange, mix in spices, or change out the type of chocolate chips.

1	cup (2 sticks) butter, melted, divided use
2^1/$_2$	cups finely crushed crisp shortbread or sugar cookie crumbs
1	cup sugar
1	5-ounce can evaporated milk (about ^{2}/$_3$ cup)
1	10-ounce package miniature marshmallows
2	cups white chocolate chips
^{3}/$_4$	teaspoon almond extract
2	teaspoons grated orange zest
1	cup chopped dried apricots
^{1}/$_2$	cup sliced almonds, skillet toasted (see page 8)

◆ Foil-line a 13x9x2-inch baking pan (see page 12); set aside.

◆ In a small saucepan melt ^{3}/$_4$ cup (1^1/$_2$ sticks) of the butter. In a medium bowl mix the melted butter and shortbread cookie crumbs. With a large square of wax paper, press mixture into bottom of prepared pan. Chill while preparing topping.

◆ In a large saucepan place the sugar, evaporated milk, marshmallows, and remaining ^{1}/$_4$ cup (^{1}/$_2$ stick) butter. Cook and stir over medium heat until mixture comes to boil, stirring constantly. Boil 5 minutes, stirring constantly. Remove from heat and add the white chocolate chips, almond extract, and orange zest, stirring until chips are completely melted.

Cookie Bars

TOASTED ALMOND-APRICOT TRUFFLE BARS

◆ Pour the chocolate mixture over the crust, spreading evenly to cover. Sprinkle with the apricots and almonds; press lightly into white chocolate layer. Refrigerate 2 hours or until firm. Cut into 36 bars. Store in covered containers between layers of wax paper. ◆ Makes 36 bars.

Icebox Bars

Cheesecake Bars

A silky layer of vanilla cream cheese atop a buttery cookie crust makes for one fine bar cookie.

1¹/₄	**cups crisp sugar cookie crumbs**
¹/₄	**cup (¹/₂ stick) butter, melted**
¹/₂	**cup milk**
2	**teaspoons unflavored gelatin**
1	**8-ounce package cream cheese, softened**
1	**cup sour cream**
³/₄	**cup powdered sugar**
1¹/₂	**teaspoons vanilla extract**

◆ Line an 8x8x2-inch baking pan with foil (see page 12); lightly spray with nonstick cooking spray. Set aside.

◆ In a medium bowl combine the sugar cookie crumbs and melted butter with a fork or fingers until well blended. Transfer crumb mixture to prepared pan. Press firmly into bottom of pan with a large square of wax paper. Freeze until ready to use.

◆ Place the milk in a small saucepan; sprinkle gelatin over (do not stir). Let stand 10 minutes to soften. Turn the heat under saucepan to medium. Whisk and stir until milk is very hot (but not boiling) and gelatin is completely dissolved. Remove from heat and set aside momentarily.

◆ In a large bowl beat the cream cheese, sour cream, powdered sugar, and vanilla with electric mixer on medium speed until creamy. Gradually add gelatin-milk mixture, beating on low speed and occasionally scraping sides of bowl with rubber spatula, until well blended.

◆ Pour and evenly spread cream cheese mixture over prepared crust. Refrigerate 3 hours or until firm. Use foil lining to remove uncut bars from pan to cutting board. Cut into 16 bars. Store, loosely covered with foil or plastic wrap, in refrigerator. ◆ Makes 16 bars.

Icebox Bars

Milk Chocolate Cheesecake Bars

Dedicated chocolate fans will delight in this quick, handheld version of chocolate cheesecake.

1$^1/_4$	cups chocolate wafer cookie crumbs
$^1/_4$	cup ($^1/_2$ stick) butter, melted
$^1/_4$	cup milk
2	teaspoons unflavored gelatin
1	8-ounce package cream cheese, softened
$^1/_2$	cup unsweetened cocoa powder
1	cup sour cream
$^3/_4$	cup powdered sugar
1	teaspoon vanilla extract

◆ Line an 8x8x2-inch baking pan with foil (see page 12); lightly spray with nonstick cooking spray. Set aside.

◆ In a medium bowl combine the chocolate cookie crumbs and melted butter with a fork or fingers until well blended. Transfer crumb mixture to prepared pan. Press firmly into bottom of pan with a large square of wax paper. Freeze until ready to use.

◆ Place the milk in a small saucepan; sprinkle gelatin over (do not stir). Let stand 10 minutes to soften. Turn the heat under saucepan to medium. Whisk and stir until milk is very hot (but not boiling) and gelatin is completely dissolved. Remove from heat and set aside momentarily.

◆ In a large bowl beat the cream cheese, sour cream, cocoa powder, powdered sugar, and vanilla with electric mixer on medium speed until creamy. Gradually add gelatin-milk mixture, beating on low speed and occasionally scraping sides of bowl with rubber spatula, until well blended.

Icebox Bars

◆ Pour and evenly spread cream cheese mixture over prepared crust. Refrigerate 3 hours or until firm. Use foil lining to remove uncut bars from pan to cutting board. Cut into 16 bars. Store, loosely covered with foil or plastic wrap, in refrigerator. ◆ Makes 16 bars.

Toffee Cheesecake Bars

Chopped English toffee candy bars and brown sugar create a new and enticing twist on cheesecake. Don't expect leftovers!

1^1/$_4$	cups crisp sugar cookie crumbs
^{1}/$_4$	cup (^{1}/$_2$ stick) butter, melted
^{1}/$_2$	cup milk
2	teaspoons unflavored gelatin
^{1}/$_2$	cup packed dark brown sugar
1	8-ounce package cream cheese, softened
1	cup sour cream
1	teaspoon vanilla extract
4	chocolate-covered English toffee bars, chopped

◆ Line an 8x8x2-inch baking pan with foil (see page 12); lightly spray with nonstick cooking spray. Set aside.

◆ In a medium bowl combine the sugar cookie crumbs and melted butter with a fork or fingers until well blended. Transfer crumb mixture to prepared pan. Press firmly into bottom of pan with a large square of wax paper. Freeze until ready to use.

◆ Place the milk in a small saucepan; sprinkle gelatin over (do not stir). Let stand 10 minutes to soften. Add the brown sugar to the saucepan. Turn the heat under saucepan to medium. Whisk and stir until milk is very hot (but not boiling) and gelatin is completely dissolved. Remove from heat and set aside momentarily.

◆ In a large bowl beat the cream cheese, sour cream, and vanilla with electric mixer on medium speed until creamy. Gradually add gelatin-milk mixture, beating on low speed and occasionally scraping sides of bowl with rubber

Icebox Bars

TOFFEE CHEESECAKE BARS

spatula, until well blended. Stir in all but about 2 tablespoons of the toffee bars to the cheesecake mixture.

◆ Pour and evenly spread cream cheese mixture over prepared crust; sprinkle remaining toffee over bars. Refrigerate 3 hours or until firm. Use foil lining to remove uncut bars from pan to cutting board. Cut into 16 bars. Store, loosely covered with foil or plastic wrap, in refrigerator. ◆ Makes 16 bars.

Icebox Bars
TOFFEE CHEESECAKE BARS

Irish Cream Mousse Bars

These petite and pretty treats are special enough to stand in for dessert under any circumstances.

2	cups crushed creme-filled chocolate sandwich cookies (about 24 cookies)
$^1/_3$	cup butter, melted
$^1/_2$	cup milk, divided use
$2^1/_4$	teaspoons unflavored gelatin
$^1/_3$	cup sugar
3	tablespoons Irish Cream liqueur
$^1/_2$	cup heavy whipping cream

❖ Line an 8x8x2-inch baking pan with foil (see page 12); lightly spray with nonstick cooking spray. Set aside.

❖ In a medium bowl combine the cookie crumbs and melted butter with a fork or fingers until well blended. Transfer crumb mixture to prepared pan. Press firmly into bottom of pan with a large square of wax paper. Freeze until ready to use.

❖ Place $^1/_4$ cup of the milk in a small saucepan. Sprinkle gelatin over milk (do not stir). Let stand 5 minutes to soften. Add sugar and remaining $^1/_4$ cup milk to saucepan. Cook and stir over low heat 4–6 minutes, until both the sugar and gelatin are dissolved. Remove from heat and stir in liqueur. Let cool 20–25 minutes until room temperature.

❖ In a medium bowl beat the whipping cream with an electric mixer set on high speed until soft peaks form. Gently stir in cooled Irish Cream mixture until just blended. Pour mixture over chilled crust. Refrigerate at least 1 hour until firm. Use foil lining to remove uncut bars from pan to cutting board. Cut into 24

small squares. Store, loosely covered with plastic wrap, in the refrigerator. ❖
Makes 24 cookies.

Variations:

Kahlua Mocha Mousse Bars: Prepare as directed above but substitute Kahlua liqueur for the Irish cream and add $1\frac{1}{2}$ teaspoons instant coffee or espresso powder to the milk mixture along with the sugar.

Grand Marnier Orange Mousse Bars: Prepare as directed above but substitute Grand Marnier or other orange liqueur for the Irish cream and use vanilla creme-filled sandwich cookies in place of the chocolate sandwich cookies.

Orange Buttercream Bars

The mild bitterness of orange zest and a deep chocolate crust temper the sweetness of these easy, creamy bars. You can prepare these sophisticated treats up to a day ahead.

$2/3$	cup plus 1 tablespoon butter, softened, divided use
$1^1/4$	cups finely crushed chocolate wafer cookies
$1^1/2$	cups powdered sugar
1	tablespoon freshly grated orange zest
1	tablespoon milk
1	teaspoon vanilla extract
1	tablespoon unsweetened cocoa

❖ Line an 8x8x2-inch baking pan with foil (see page 12); lightly spray with nonstick cooking spray. Set aside.

❖ In a small saucepan set over low heat, melt $1/3$ cup butter. In a medium bowl combine the melted butter and cookie crumbs until blended. Transfer crumb mixture to prepared pan. Press firmly into bottom of pan with a large square of wax paper. Freeze until ready to use.

❖ In a medium bowl beat the powdered sugar, orange zest, milk, vanilla, and $1/3$ cup of the remaining softened butter with an electric mixer set on medium speed until creamy. Spread filling mixture over prepared crust.

❖ In a small saucepan set over low heat, melt the remaining 1 tablespoon butter. Remove from heat and whisk in cocoa powder until blended and smooth. Drizzle over filling. Refrigerate bars until firm, about 1–2 hours. Use foil lining to remove uncut bars from pan to cutting board. Cut into 16 bars. Store, loosely covered with plastic wrap, in the refrigerator. ❖ Makes 16 bars.

Icebox Bars

Coconut Lime Bars

The mesmerizing melding of lime and coconut is captured in these silky treats.
The dynamic flavor duo is made even dreamier with a coconut cookie crust.

1$^1/_4$	**cups crisp macaroon cookie crumbs**
$^1/_4$	**cup ($^1/_2$ stick) butter, melted**
1	**6-ounce container frozen limeade concentrate, thawed**
2	**teaspoons unflavored gelatin**
1	**cup unsweetened coconut milk, chilled**
1	**8-ounce package cream cheese, softened**

◆ Line an 8x8x2-inch baking pan with foil (see page 12); lightly spray with nonstick cooking spray. Set aside.

◆ In a medium bowl combine the cookie crumbs and melted butter with a fork or fingers until well blended. Transfer crumb mixture to prepared pan. Press firmly into bottom of pan with a large square of wax paper. Freeze until ready to use.

◆ Place the limeade concentrate in a small saucepan; sprinkle gelatin over (do not stir). Let stand 5 minutes to soften. Turn heat under saucepan to medium and whisk until mixture is hot but not boiling and gelatin is completely dissolved; let cool 20 minutes.

◆ In a large bowl beat the coconut milk and cream cheese with electric mixer on medium speed until blended and smooth. Gradually add lime mixture, beating until well blended.

◆ Pour and evenly spread mixture over prepared crust. Refrigerate 3 hours or until firm. Use foil lining to remove uncut bars from pan to cutting board. Cut into 16 bars. Store, loosely covered with plastic wrap, in the refrigerator. ◆ Makes 16 bars.

Apricot Mousse Bars

Delicate and lovely, these light and creamy bars are one-of-a-kind. If you like, substitute canned peaches or fresh mangoes for the apricots.

2	cups crushed creme-filled lemon sandwich cookies (about 24 cookies)
$^1/_3$	cup butter, melted
1	cup canned, drained apricot halves
$^1/_2$	cup orange juice, divided use
$2^1/_4$	teaspoons unflavored gelatin
$^1/_3$	cup sugar
$^2/_3$	cup heavy whipping cream

◆ Line an 8x8x2-inch baking pan with foil (see page 12); lightly spray with nonstick cooking spray. Set aside.

◆ In a medium bowl combine the cookie crumbs and melted butter with a fork or fingers until well blended. Transfer crumb mixture to prepared pan. Press firmly into bottom of pan with a large square of wax paper. Freeze until ready to use.

◆ In a blender or food processor puree the apricots with $^1/_4$ cup of the orange juice; set aside.

◆ Place the remaining $^1/_4$ cup orange juice in a small saucepan. Sprinkle gelatin over (do not stir). Let stand 5 minutes to soften. Add sugar and apricot puree to saucepan. Cook and stir over low heat 4–6 minutes until both the sugar and gelatin are dissolved. Remove from heat. Let cool 20–25 minutes until room temperature.

◆ In a medium bowl beat the whipping cream with an electric mixer set on high speed until soft peaks form. Gently stir in cooled apricot mixture until just blended. Pour mixture over chilled crust. Refrigerate 3 hours until firm. Use foil lining to remove uncut bars from pan to cutting board. Cut into 24 small squares. Store, loosely covered with plastic wrap, in the refrigerator. ◈ Makes 24 cookies.

Icebox Bars
APRICOT MOUSSE BARS

Key Lime Bars

Add some sophisticated, citrus flair to your next cookout with this cool bar cookie, which showcases a tart-sweet lime filling and a buttery vanilla crust.

2	cups crushed creme-filled vanilla sandwich cookies (about 24 cookies)
$^1/_3$	cup butter, melted
2	teaspoons unflavored gelatin
$^1/_2$	cup Key lime or regular lime juice
1	14-ounce can sweetened condensed milk
1	teaspoon grated lime zest
$^1/_2$	cup chilled heavy whipping cream
	Fresh lime slices (optional—for garnish)

◆ Line a 9x9x2-inch baking pan with foil (see page 12); lightly spray with nonstick cooking spray. Set aside.

◆ In a medium bowl combine the cookie crumbs and melted butter with a fork or fingers until well blended. Transfer crumb mixture to prepared pan. Press firmly into bottom of pan with a large square of wax paper. Freeze until ready to use.

◆ In a medium bowl sprinkle gelatin over the lime juice; let stand 5 minutes. Heat over low heat, stirring until gelatin dissolves. Pour the juice into a large bowl; whisk in sweetened condensed milk and grated lime zest.

◆ Place bowl in a larger bowl filled with ice; whisk mixture 10 minutes or until partially set. In a medium bowl beat the whipping cream with an electric mixer set on high speed until soft peaks form. Fold whipped cream into lime mixture.

Icebox Bars

KEY LIME BARS

Pour evenly over prepared crust; cover and chill 8 hours. Use foil lining to remove uncut bars from pan to cutting board. Cut into 24 bars. Garnish with lime slices, if desired. Store, loosely covered with plastic wrap, in the refrigerator. ❖ Makes 24 bars.

Grasshopper Bars

Not a mint fan? Customize these gourmet, grown-up bars with the liqueur of your choice. The bars will be impressive and delicious no matter which flavor you choose.

1¹/₄	cups chocolate wafer cookie crumbs
¹/₄	cup (¹/₂ stick) butter, melted
¹/₃	cup crème de menthe liqueur
2	teaspoons unflavored gelatin
²/₃	cup heavy whipping cream
1	8-ounce package cream cheese, softened
³/₄	cup powdered sugar
¹/₂	cup miniature semisweet chocolate chips

◆ Line an 8x8x2-inch baking pan with foil (see page 12); lightly spray with nonstick cooking spray. Set aside.

◆ In a medium bowl combine the cookie crumbs and melted butter with a fork or fingers until well blended. Transfer crumb mixture to prepared pan. Press firmly into bottom of pan with a large square of wax paper. Freeze until ready to use.

◆ Place the liqueur in a small cup; sprinkle gelatin over (do not stir). Let stand 5 minutes to soften.

◆ In a small saucepan set over medium heat, heat the cream until hot but not boiling. Add the gelatin mixture. Whisk and stir until gelatin is completely dissolved. Remove from heat and set aside momentarily.

◆ In a large bowl beat the cream cheese and powdered sugar with electric mixer on medium speed until creamy. Gradually add gelatin-cream mixture,

Icebox Bars

beating on low speed and occasionally scraping sides of bowl with rubber spatula, until well blended.

◆ Pour and evenly spread cream cheese mixture over prepared crust; sprinkle with chocolate chips. Refrigerate 3 hours or until firm. Use foil lining to remove uncut bars from pan to cutting board. Cut into 16 bars. Store, loosely covered with foil or plastic wrap, in refrigerator. ◆ Makes 16 bars.

Ambrosia Bars

Consider cutting this cookie version of the "food of the gods" into diamonds or triangles to create little works of arts on your cookie tray.

1$^1/_4$	cups crisp macaroon cookie crumbs
$^1/_4$	cup ($^1/_2$ stick) butter, melted
$^2/_3$	cup canned unsweetened coconut milk
2	teaspoons unflavored gelatin
1	8-ounce package cream cheese, softened
1	6-ounce container frozen orange juice concentrate, thawed
1	cup sweetened flake coconut
$^1/_2$	cup coarsely chopped maraschino cherries

◆ Line an 8x8x2-inch baking pan with foil (see page 12); lightly spray with nonstick cooking spray. Set aside.

◆ In a medium bowl combine the cookie crumbs and melted butter with a fork or fingers until well blended. Transfer crumb mixture to prepared pan. Press firmly into bottom of pan with a large square of wax paper. Freeze until ready to use.

◆ Place $^1/_3$ cup of the coconut milk in a small saucepan; sprinkle gelatin over (do not stir). Let stand 10 minutes to soften. Add the remaining $^1/_3$ cup coconut milk to saucepan and turn the heat under saucepan to medium. Whisk and stir until coconut milk is very hot (but not boiling) and gelatin is completely dissolved. Remove from heat and cool 15 minutes.

◆ In a large bowl beat the cream cheese and thawed orange juice concentrate with electric mixer on medium speed until creamy. Gradually add gelatin mixture, beating on low speed and occasionally scraping sides of bowl with rubber spatula, until well blended.

Icebox Bars

AMBROSIA BARS

◆ Pour and evenly spread filling over prepared crust. Sprinkle coconut and cherries over bars, pressing gently into filling. Refrigerate 3 hours or until firm. Use foil lining to remove uncut bars from pan to cutting board. Cut into 16 bars. Store, loosely covered with foil or plastic wrap, in refrigerator. ◆ Makes 16 bars.

Icebox Bars
AMBROSIA BARS

Triple Chocolate Pudding Bars

Elevate your sense of well-being and euphoria with these voluptuous chocolate bars.

5	tablespoons butter, divided use
$1^1/_4$	cups chocolate wafer cookie crumbs
$4^1/_2$	tablespoons cornstarch
$^2/_3$	cup sugar
$^1/_3$	cup unsweetened cocoa powder
2	cups half and half
$^2/_3$	cup semisweet chocolate chips

◆ Line an 8x8x2-inch baking pan with foil (see page 12); lightly spray with nonstick cooking spray. Set aside.

◆ Melt 4 tablespoons ($^1/_2$ stick) of the butter in a large nonstick skillet set over medium-high heat. In a medium bowl combine the cookie crumbs and melted butter with a fork or fingers until well blended. Transfer crumb mixture to prepared pan. Press firmly into bottom of pan with a large square of wax paper. Freeze until ready to use.

◆ In a medium saucepan combine the cornstarch, sugar, and cocoa powder. Whisk in 1 cup of the half and half until smooth and blended; whisk in remaining half and half. Cook and stir over medium high heat until mixture is thick and bubbly.

◆ Remove pan from heat; whisk in chocolate chips and remaining tablespoon butter until chips are melted and mixture is smooth. Let cool 20 minutes. Pour mixture over prepared crust, smoothing top with a rubber spatula. Place a piece of plastic wrap directly on filling. Refrigerate 4–6 hours or until firm. Cut into 16 bars. Use foil lining to remove uncut bars from pan to cutting board. Store, loosely covered with foil or plastic wrap, in refrigerator. ◆ Makes 16 bars.

Icebox Bars

Blueberry Bars

Showcase plump, fresh blueberries in these gorgeous bars during the summer months, or make them year-round with frozen berries. Either way, you're sure to receive rave reviews.

1 $^1/_4$	cups crisp sugar cookie crumbs
$^1/_4$	cup ($^1/_2$ stick) butter, melted
3	tablespoons fresh lemon juice
2 $^1/_4$	teaspoons unflavored gelatin
1 $^1/_2$	cups fresh blueberries or frozen (thawed) blueberries
$^1/_2$	cup sugar
1	8-ounce package cream cheese, softened

◆ Line an 8x8x2-inch baking pan with foil (see page 12); lightly spray with nonstick cooking spray. Set aside.

◆ In a medium bowl combine the cookie crumbs and melted butter with a fork or fingers until well blended. Transfer crumb mixture to prepared pan. Press firmly into bottom of pan with a large square of wax paper. Freeze until ready to use.

◆ Place the lemon juice in a small cup; sprinkle gelatin over (do not stir). Let stand 5 minutes to soften.

◆ Puree the blueberries and sugar in a blender or food processor until smooth. Transfer mixture to a small saucepan. Heat over medium-high heat until hot but not boiling. Add gelatin mixture to saucepan. Whisk until gelatin is completely dissolved. Remove from heat and cool 20 minutes.

◆ In a large bowl beat the cream cheese with electric mixer on medium speed until creamy. Gradually add blueberry mixture, beating until well blended. Pour and evenly spread over prepared crust. Refrigerate 3 hours or until firm. Use foil lining to remove uncut bars from pan to cutting board. Cut into 16 bars. Store, loosely covered with foil or plastic wrap, in refrigerator. ◆ Makes 16 bars.

Icebox Bars
BLUEBERRY BARS

Sour Cream Lemon Bars

Light and refreshing, these tangy citrus bars are a great finale for a warm weather supper.

2	cups crushed creme-filled lemon sandwich cookies (about 24 cookies)
$^1/_3$	cup butter, melted
2	teaspoons unflavored gelatin
$^1/_2$	cup fresh lemon juice, divided use
1	3-ounce package cream cheese, softened
$1^1/_3$	cups sour cream
$1^1/_2$	teaspoons freshly grated lemon zest
1	cup powdered sugar

◆ Line an 8x8x2-inch baking pan with foil (see page 12); lightly spray with nonstick cooking spray. Set aside.

◆ In a medium bowl combine the cookie crumbs and melted butter with a fork or fingers until well blended. Transfer crumb mixture to prepared pan. Press firmly into bottom of pan with a large square of wax paper. Freeze until ready to use.

◆ Place $^1/_4$ cup of the lemon juice in a small saucepan; sprinkle gelatin over (do not stir). Let stand 5 minutes to soften.

◆ Add the remaining $^1/_4$ cup lemon juice to saucepan and turn heat to medium. Whisk until hot but not boiling and gelatin is completely dissolved. Let cool 15 minutes.

◆ In a large bowl beat the cream cheese, sour cream, lemon zest, and powdered sugar with electric mixer on medium speed until creamy. Gradually add lemon

Icebox Bars

mixture, beating until well blended. Pour and evenly spread over prepared crust. Refrigerate 3 hours or until firm. Use foil lining to remove uncut bars from pan to cutting board. Cut into 16 bars. Store, loosely covered with foil or plastic wrap, in refrigerator. ◆ Makes 16 bars.

Icebox Bars

SOUR CREAM LEMON BARS

Eggnog Bars

Rich with rum and spiced with nutmeg, these bars will be a surefire hit with holiday revelers.

2	cups crushed creme-filled vanilla sandwich cookies (about 24 cookies)
$^1/_3$	cup butter, melted
1	teaspoon ground cinnamon
$^1/_4$	cup dark rum
2	teaspoons unflavored gelatin
1	cup chilled eggnog, divided use
1	8-ounce package cream cheese, softened
$^2/_3$	cup powdered sugar
$^1/_4$	teaspoon ground nutmeg

◆ Line an 8x8x2-inch baking pan with foil (see page 12); lightly spray with nonstick cooking spray. Set aside.

◆ In a medium bowl combine the cookie crumbs, melted butter, and cinnamon with a fork or fingers until well blended. Transfer crumb mixture to prepared pan. Press firmly into bottom of pan with a large square of wax paper. Freeze until ready to use.

◆ Place the rum in a small saucepan; sprinkle gelatin over (do not stir). Let stand 5 minutes to soften.

◆ Add $^1/_4$ cup eggnog to saucepan and turn heat to medium. Whisk until hot but not boiling and gelatin is completely dissolved. Remove from heat and whisk in remaining eggnog. Let cool 5 minutes.

◆ In a large bowl beat the cream cheese, powdered sugar, and nutmeg with

Icebox Bars
EGGNOG BARS

electric mixer on medium speed until creamy and smooth. Gradually add gelatin mixture, beating until well blended. Pour and evenly spread over prepared crust. Refrigerate 3 hours or until firm. Use foil lining to remove uncut bars from pan to cutting board. Cut into 16 bars. Store, loosely covered with foil or plastic wrap, in refrigerator. ◆ Makes 16 bars.

Icebox Bars
EGGNOG BARS

Blackberry Mascarpone Bars

Extra rich and creamy mascarpone, a soft Italian cheese similar to cream cheese, teams up with the bright flavor of fresh blackberries in these stylish cookies. If mascarpone is unavailable, substitute one 8-ounce package of cream cheese.

1$^1/_4$	cups crisp sugar cookie crumbs
$^1/_4$	cup ($^1/_2$ stick) butter, melted
$^1/_2$	cup milk
2$^1/_4$	teaspoons unflavored gelatin
1	8-ounce container mascarpone cheese, room temperature
$^1/_2$	cup sour cream
$^3/_4$	cup powdered sugar
1	teaspoon vanilla extract
$^1/_4$	teaspoon ground cardamom
1	cup fresh blackberries

◆ Line an 8x8x2-inch baking pan with foil (see page 12); lightly spray with nonstick cooking spray. Set aside.

◆ In a medium bowl combine the cookie crumbs and melted butter with a fork or fingers until well blended. Transfer crumb mixture to prepared pan. Press firmly into bottom of pan with a large square of wax paper. Freeze until ready to use.

◆ Place the milk in a small saucepan; sprinkle gelatin over (do not stir). Let stand 10 minutes to soften. Turn the heat under saucepan to medium. Whisk and stir until milk is very hot (but not boiling) and gelatin is completely dissolved. Remove from heat and set aside momentarily.

◆ In a large bowl beat the mascarpone cheese, sour cream, powdered sugar, vanilla, and cardamom with electric mixer on medium speed until creamy.

Icebox Bars

Gradually add gelatin-milk mixture, beating on low speed and occasionally scraping sides of bowl with rubber spatula, until well blended.

❖ Pour and evenly spread mascarpone mixture over prepared crust. Press the blackberries into the top of the bars. Refrigerate 3 hours or until firm. Use foil lining to remove uncut bars from pan to cutting board. Cut into 16 bars. Store, loosely covered with foil or plastic wrap, in refrigerator. ❖ Makes 16 bars.

Icebox Bars
BLACKBERRY MASCARPONE BARS

Margarita Bars

If you're looking for an all-out summertime dazzler, these margarita-inspired bars, with their salty-sweet crust and cool lime and orange filling, will fit the bill.

1¹/₃	cups crushed pretzels
¹/₄	cup (¹/₂ stick) butter, melted
2	tablespoons sugar
¹/₄	cup lime juice
2	teaspoons unflavored gelatin
¹/₄	cup orange juice
1¹/₂	teaspoons freshly grated lime zest
1	8-ounce package cream cheese, softened
¹/₂	cup sour cream
³/₄	cup powdered sugar
3	tablespoons tequila

◆ Line an 8x8x2-inch baking pan with foil (see page 12); lightly spray with nonstick cooking spray. Set aside.

◆ In a medium bowl combine the pretzel crumbs, melted butter, and sugar with a fork or fingers until well blended. Transfer crumb mixture to prepared pan. Press firmly into bottom of pan with a large square of wax paper. Freeze until ready to use.

◆ Place the lime juice in a small saucepan; sprinkle gelatin over (do not stir). Let stand 10 minutes to soften. Add the orange juice to the saucepan and turn the heat under saucepan to medium. Whisk and stir until juice mixture is very hot (but not boiling) and gelatin is completely dissolved. Remove from heat and set aside momentarily.

◆ In a large bowl beat the lime zest, cream cheese, sour cream, powdered sugar, and tequila with electric mixer on medium speed until creamy. Gradually

Icebox Bars

add gelatin mixture, beating on low speed and occasionally scraping sides of bowl with rubber spatula, until well blended.

◆ Pour and evenly spread the filling over prepared crust. Refrigerate 3 hours or until firm. Use foil lining to remove uncut bars from pan to cutting board. Cut into 16 bars. Store, loosely covered with foil or plastic wrap, in refrigerator. ◆ Makes 16 bars.

Icebox Bars
MARGARITA BARS

Honey-Sour Cream Bars

Summer days fly swiftly by, but you can make the most of them by savoring these cool, honey-laced sour cream bars. Add a few tall glasses of iced tea, a handful of good friends, and you're all set.

1¼	cups crisp sugar cookie crumbs
¼	cup (½ stick) butter, melted
⅓	cup milk
2	teaspoons unflavored gelatin
⅓	cup honey
1	16-ounce container sour cream
1	teaspoon vanilla extract
¼	teaspoon ground coriander or nutmeg

◇ Line an 8x8x2-inch baking pan with foil (see page 12); lightly spray with nonstick cooking spray. Set aside.

◇ In a medium bowl combine the cookie crumbs and melted butter with a fork or fingers until well blended. Transfer crumb mixture to prepared pan. Press firmly into bottom of pan with a large square of wax paper. Freeze until ready to use.

◇ Place the milk in a small saucepan; sprinkle gelatin over (do not stir). Let stand 10 minutes to soften. Turn the heat under saucepan to medium. Whisk and stir until milk is very hot (but not boiling) and gelatin is completely dissolved. Remove from heat and cool 15 minutes.

◇ In a medium bowl whisk the honey, sour cream, vanilla, and coriander until blended and smooth. Gradually whisk in the cooled gelatin-milk mixture until well blended.

Icebox Bars

◆ Pour and evenly spread sour cream mixture over prepared crust. Refrigerate 3 hours or until firm. Use foil lining to remove uncut bars from pan to cutting board. Cut into 16 bars. Store, loosely covered with foil or plastic wrap, in refrigerator. ◆ Makes 16 bars.

Icebox Bars
HONEY–SOUR CREAM BARS

White Chocolate Berry Bars

Trust me—it's never a mistake to serve a white chocolate–raspberry confection for dessert.

2	cups crushed creme-filled vanilla sandwich cookies (about 24 cookies)
$^1/_3$	cup butter, melted
$^1/_2$	cup heavy whipping cream
2	teaspoons unflavored gelatin
1	cup white chocolate chips
1	cup sour cream
1	cup fresh blueberries, raspberries, or blackberries

❖ Line an 8x8x2-inch pan with foil (see page 12). Lightly coat foil with non-stick cooking spray.

❖ In a medium bowl combine the cookie crumbs and melted butter with a fork or fingers until well blended. Transfer crumb mixture to prepared pan. Press firmly into bottom of pan with a large square of wax paper. Freeze until ready to use.

❖ Place the cream in a small saucepan. Sprinkle gelatin over cream (do not stir). Let stand 5 minutes to soften. Cook and stir over low heat 4–6 minutes until cream is hot (but not boiling) and gelatin is dissolved. Remove from heat and add white chocolate chips; stir until melted and smooth. Set aside and let cool 20–25 minutes until room temperature.

❖ In a medium bowl whisk the sour cream and white chocolate mixture until blended and smooth. Pour and evenly spread mixture over chilled crust. Sprinkle berries over surface of bars and gently press into filling. Refrigerate at least 3 hours until firm. Use foil lining to remove uncut bars from pan to cutting board. Cut into 16 bars. Store, loosely covered with foil or plastic wrap, in refrigerator. ❖ Makes 16 bars.

Icebox Bars

Gianduia Bars

The rich chocolate-hazelnut flavor of these European-inspired cookies qualifies them as classic. Plus, they're practically foolproof, a fact appreciated by cooks of all experience levels.

2	cups crushed creme-filled chocolate sandwich cookies (about 24 cookies)
$1/3$	cup butter, melted
$1/2$	cup heavy whipping cream
2	teaspoons unflavored gelatin
$2/3$	cup semisweet chocolate chips
1	13-ounce jar chocolate-hazelnut spread (e.g., Nutella)

◆ Line an 8x8x2-inch pan with foil (see page 12). Lightly coat foil with non-stick cooking spray.

◆ In a medium bowl combine the cookie crumbs and melted butter with a fork or fingers until well blended. Transfer crumb mixture to prepared pan. Press firmly into bottom of pan with a large square of wax paper. Freeze until ready to use.

◆ Place cream in a small saucepan. Sprinkle gelatin over cream (do not stir). Let stand 5 minutes to soften. Cook and stir over low heat 4–6 minutes until cream is hot (but not boiling) and gelatin is dissolved. Remove from heat and add chocolate chips; stir until melted and smooth. Add chocolate-hazelnut spread to mixture; whisk until blended and smooth. Set aside and let cool 15–20 minutes until room temperature.

◆ Pour and evenly spread filling over chilled crust. Refrigerate at least 3 hours until firm. Use foil lining to remove uncut bars from pan to cutting board. Cut into 16 bars. Store, loosely covered with foil or plastic wrap, in refrigerator. ◆ Makes 16 bars.

Italian Cheesecake Bars

A splash of Marsala wine, a sprinkle of lemon zest, and a buttery shortbread crust add up to one decadent bar.

1$^1/_4$	cups crisp sugar cookie crumbs
$^1/_4$	cup ($^1/_2$ stick) butter, melted
$^1/_4$	cup Marsala or sweet Sherry wine
2	teaspoons unflavored gelatin
$^1/_4$	cup orange juice
1	3-ounce package cream cheese, softened
1	8-ounce container ricotta cheese
$^3/_4$	cup powdered sugar
1	teaspoon vanilla extract
$^2/_3$	cup golden raisins
$^1/_2$	cup sliced almonds, skillet-toasted (see page 8) (optional)

◆ Line an 8x8x2-inch baking pan with foil (see page 12); lightly spray with nonstick cooking spray. Set aside.

◆ In a medium bowl combine the cookie crumbs and melted butter with a fork or fingers until well blended. Transfer crumb mixture to prepared pan. Press firmly into bottom of pan with a large square of wax paper. Freeze until ready to use.

◆ Place the Marsala in a small saucepan; sprinkle gelatin over (do not stir). Let stand 10 minutes to soften. Add the orange juice to saucepan and turn the heat under saucepan to medium. Whisk and stir until liquid is very hot (but not boiling) and gelatin is completely dissolved. Remove from heat and cool 15 minutes.

❖ In a large bowl beat the cream cheese, ricotta cheese, powdered sugar, and vanilla with electric mixer on medium speed until creamy. Gradually add cooled gelatin mixture, beating on low speed and occasionally scraping sides of bowl with rubber spatula, until well blended. Stir in golden raisins.

❖ Pour and evenly spread cheese mixture over prepared crust. Sprinkle top of bars with toasted almonds, if desired. Refrigerate 3 hours or until firm. Use foil lining to remove uncut bars from pan to cutting board. Cut into 16 bars. Store, loosely covered with foil or plastic wrap, in refrigerator. ❖ Makes 16 bars.

Icebox Bars
ITALIAN CHEESECAKE BARS

Pink Lemonade Squares

A smooth texture and tart lemon flavor make these bars a great follow-up to a spicy meal, whether Indian curry or Texas BBQ.

1¼	cups crisp sugar cookie crumbs
¼	cup (1/2 stick) butter, melted
1	8-ounce package cream cheese, softened
1	cup jarred marshmallow creme
2	tablespoons fresh lemon juice
2	teaspoons grated lemon zest
1–2	drops red food coloring

◆ Line an 8x8x2-inch baking pan with foil (see page 12); lightly spray with nonstick cooking spray. Set aside.

◆ In a medium bowl combine the cookie crumbs and melted butter with a fork or fingers until well blended. Transfer crumb mixture to prepared pan. Press firmly into bottom of pan with a large square of wax paper. Freeze until ready to use.

◆ In a medium bowl beat the cream cheese, marshmallow creme, lemon juice, lemon zest, and enough red food coloring to tint mixture pale pink with electric mixer set on medium until light and fluffy. Spread evenly over crust.

◆ Refrigerate at least 4 hours until firm. Use foil lining to remove uncut bars from pan to cutting board. Cut into 16 squares. Store, loosely covered with foil or plastic wrap, in refrigerator. ◆ Makes 16 squares.

Icebox Bars

Turtle Cheesecake Bars

Here pecans, caramel, and chocolate transform a simple cheesecake bar into an extraordinary treat.

2¹/₂	cups chocolate wafer cookie crumbs
3	tablespoons sugar
¹/₂	cup (1 stick) butter, melted
¹/₂	cup chopped pecans
2	8-ounce packages cream cheese, softened
1¹/₂	cups cold milk
¹/₄	cup firmly packed dark brown sugar
1	4-serving-size package instant butterscotch pudding and pie filling mix
²/₃	cup caramel ice cream topping
1	cup pecan halves

◆ Line a 13x9x2-inch baking pan with foil (see page 12); lightly spray with nonstick cooking spray. Set aside.

◆ In a medium bowl combine the cookie crumbs, sugar, melted butter, and pecans with a fork or fingers until well blended. Transfer crumb mixture to prepared pan. Press firmly into bottom of pan with a large square of wax paper. Freeze until ready to use.

◆ In a large bowl beat the cream cheese with an electric mixer set on medium-high speed until light and fluffy. Gradually beat in the milk until smooth and well blended. Add the brown sugar and pudding mix; beat at low speed for 2 minutes. Pour and evenly spread mixture over crust in pan.

◆ Drizzle with caramel topping; swirl into filling with tip of knife. Arrange pecan halves over top of cheesecake. Refrigerate at least 3 hours or until firm. Use foil lining to remove uncut bars from pan to cutting board. Cut into 36 bars. Store, loosely covered with foil or plastic wrap, in refrigerator. ◆ Makes 36 bars.

Icebox Bars

TURTLE CHEESECAKE BARS

Pumpkin Bars

One taste of these creamy no-bake pumpkin bars may just convince you to start a delicious new holiday dessert tradition.

1¼	cups gingersnap cookie crumbs
¼	cup (½ stick) butter, melted
⅓	cup milk
2	teaspoons unflavored gelatin
½	cup firmly packed light brown sugar
1	cup canned solid pack pumpkin
1	8-ounce package cream cheese, softened
2	teaspoons pumpkin pie spice blend
1	teaspoon vanilla extract

◆ Line an 8x8x2-inch baking pan with foil (see page 12); lightly spray with nonstick cooking spray. Set aside.

◆ In a medium bowl combine the cookie crumbs and melted butter with a fork or fingers until well blended. Transfer crumb mixture to prepared pan. Press firmly into bottom of pan with a large square of wax paper. Freeze until ready to use.

◆ Place the milk in a small saucepan; sprinkle gelatin over (do not stir). Let stand 10 minutes to soften. Add the brown sugar to saucepan and turn the heat under saucepan to medium. Whisk and stir until liquid is very hot (but not boiling) and both the gelatin and brown sugar are completely dissolved. Remove from heat and cool 15 minutes.

◆ In a large bowl beat the pumpkin, cream cheese, pumpkin pie spice, and vanilla with electric mixer on medium speed until creamy. Gradually add cooled gelatin mixture, beating on low speed and occasionally scraping sides of bowl with rubber spatula, until well blended.

Icebox Bars

PUMPKIN BARS

◆ Pour and evenly spread cheese mixture over prepared crust. Refrigerate 3 hours or until firm. Use foil lining to remove uncut bars from pan to cutting board. Cut into 16 bars. Store, loosely covered with foil or plastic wrap, in refrigerator. ◆ Makes 16 bars.

Icebox Bars
PUMPKIN BARS

Butterscotch Pudding Bars

Rich and creamy, these bars dazzle with their deep butterscotch flavor. It's a great way to enjoy the comforts of pudding in hand-held form.

11	tablespoons butter, divided use
2	cups crushed creme-filled vanilla sandwich cookies (about 24 cookies)
$1/4$	cup cornstarch
$2^1/_2$	cups half and half, divided use
$2/_3$	cup packed dark brown sugar
1	teaspoon vanilla extract

◆ Line an 8x8x2-inch baking pan with foil (see page 12); lightly spray with nonstick cooking spray. Set aside.

◆ In a large nonstick skillet set over medium-high heat, melt 6 tablespoons of the butter. In a medium bowl combine the melted butter and cookie crumbs with a fork or fingers until well blended. Transfer crumb mixture to prepared pan. Press firmly into bottom of pan with a large square of wax paper. Freeze until ready to use.

◆ In a small bowl whisk the cornstarch and $1/2$ cup of the half and half until the cornstarch is dissolved; set aside.

◆ In a medium saucepan combine the brown sugar and remaining 5 tablespoons butter. Cook over low heat, whisking constantly, until the butter is melted.

◆ Whisk in the remaining 2 cups of the half and half until smooth and blended. Add cornstarch mixture. Cook and stir over medium-high heat until mixture is thick and bubbly. Remove from heat and whisk in vanilla. Cool 20 minutes, whisking occasionally to prevent skin from forming on top.

Icebox Bars

◆ Pour and evenly spread mixture over prepared crust. Place a piece of plastic wrap directly on filling. Refrigerate 4–6 hours or until firm. Use foil lining to remove uncut bars from pan to cutting board. Cut into 16 bars. Store, loosely covered with foil or plastic wrap, in refrigerator. ◆ Makes 16 bars.

Icebox Bars
BUTTERSCOTCH PUDDING BARS

Maple Cream Bars

Fruitcake may be traditional and candies well-loved, but for a truly special holiday treat, whip up a batch of these very maple bars. Look for the maple-flavored extract in the baking aisle where vanilla extract is shelved.

1$^1/_4$	cups crisp sugar cookie crumbs
$^1/_4$	cup ($^1/_2$ stick) butter, melted
1	cup chilled heavy whipping cream, divided use
2	teaspoons unflavored gelatin
$^1/_2$	cup pure maple syrup
1	8-ounce package cream cheese, softened
1$^1/_2$	teaspoons maple-flavored extract

◆ Line an 8x8x2-inch baking pan with foil (see page 12); lightly spray with nonstick cooking spray. Set aside.

◆ In a medium bowl combine the cookie crumbs and melted butter with a fork or fingers until well blended. Transfer crumb mixture to prepared pan. Press firmly into bottom of pan with a large square of wax paper. Freeze until ready to use.

◆ Place $^1/_2$ cup of the cream in a small saucepan; sprinkle gelatin over (do not stir). Let stand 10 minutes to soften. Add the maple syrup to saucepan and turn the heat under saucepan to medium. Whisk and stir until liquid is very hot (but not boiling) and the gelatin is completely dissolved. Remove from heat and cool 15 minutes.

◆ In a medium bowl beat the maple extract and remaining $^1/_2$ cup chilled cream with electric mixer on high speed until soft peaks form; set aside momentarily.

◆ In a separate medium bowl beat the cream cheese with electric mixer on medium until light and fluffy. Gradually add gelatin-maple mixture, beating on

Icebox Bars

MAPLE CREAM BARS

low speed and occasionally scraping sides of bowl with rubber spatula, until well blended. Fold in whipped cream with a rubber spatula.

◆ Pour and evenly spread filling over prepared crust. Refrigerate 3 hours or until firm. Use foil lining to remove uncut bars from pan to cutting board. Cut into 16 bars. Store, loosely covered with foil or plastic wrap, in refrigerator. ◆ Makes 16 bars.

Raspberry Lemon Squares

Raspberries, with their ruby color and lush flavor, have so much going for them that they taste great in pies, in cake, and certainly in these lemon-laced summertime bar cookies.

2	cups fresh raspberries, divided use
1$^1/_4$	cups crisp sugar or macaroon cookie crumbs
$^1/_4$	cup ($^1/_2$ stick) butter, melted
1	8-ounce package cream cheese, softened
1	cup jarred marshmallow creme
1$^1/_2$	tablespoons fresh lemon juice
2	teaspoons grated lemon zest

◆ Line a 9x9x2-inch baking pan with foil (see page 12); lightly spray with nonstick cooking spray. Set aside.

◆ Remove 16 of the raspberries for garnish; place in refrigerator until ready to use.

◆ In a medium bowl combine the cookie crumbs and melted butter with a fork or fingers until well blended. Transfer crumb mixture to prepared pan. Press firmly into bottom of pan with a large square of wax paper. Freeze until ready to use.

◆ In a medium bowl beat the cream cheese, marshmallow creme, lemon juice, and lemon zest with electric mixer set on medium until light and fluffy. Gently fold in remaining raspberries; spread evenly over crust. Poke reserved 16 raspberries atop filling in 4x4 rows.

◆ Refrigerate at least 4 hours or until firm. Use foil lining to remove uncut bars from pan to cutting board. Cut into 16 squares with a raspberry centered in each square. Store, loosely covered with foil or plastic wrap, in refrigerator. ◆ Makes 16 squares.

Icebox Bars

Mango Cream Bars

A spicy gingersnap crust is the perfect foil for the lush, tropical filling in these bars. For an additional tropical twist, consider sprinkling the bars with $1/2$ cup sweetened flake coconut before chilling.

$1^1/_4$	cups gingersnap cookie crumbs
$^1/_4$	cup ($^1/_2$ stick) butter, melted
$^1/_4$	cup fresh lime juice
2	teaspoons unflavored gelatin
1	8-ounce package cream cheese, softened
$^2/_3$	cup powdered sugar
$1^1/_2$	teaspoons grated lime zest
1	cup chopped fresh mango (about 1 large mango)

◆ Line an 8x8x2-inch baking pan with foil (see page 12); lightly spray with nonstick cooking spray. Set aside.

◆ In a medium bowl combine the cookie crumbs and melted butter with a fork or fingers until well blended. Transfer crumb mixture to prepared pan. Press firmly into bottom of pan with a large square of wax paper. Freeze until ready to use.

◆ Pour lime juice into small saucepan; sprinkle gelatin over. Let stand 10 minutes. Stir over very low heat just until gelatin dissolves. Set aside.

◆ In a food processor or blender, blend the cream cheese, powdered sugar, lime zest, and mango until smooth. With machine running, add warm gelatin mixture; blend well. Pour and spread filling evenly over crust. Cover and chill overnight. Use foil lining to remove uncut bars from pan to cutting board. Cut into 16 bars. Store, loosely covered with foil or plastic wrap, in refrigerator. ◆ Makes 16 bars.

Chocolate Decadence Bars

Got a chocolate lover in your family or circle of friends? If so, ordinary cookies just won't cut it, but these intensely chocolate, triple-layer treats will thrill them through and through.

1	8-ounce package semisweet baking chocolate, divided use
10	tablespoons butter, divided use
1¹/₂	cups graham cracker crumbs
¹/₃	cup water
1	4-serving-size package chocolate instant pudding & pie filling
2	cups powdered sugar
¹/₂	cup heavy whipping cream

◆ Line a 9x9x2-inch baking pan with foil (see page 12); lightly spray with nonstick cooking spray. Set aside.

◆ Coarsely chop the chocolate. Place half of the chopped chocolate and 5 table-spoons of the butter in a large microwavable bowl. Microwave on high for 2 minutes or until butter is melted (chocolate will not look completely melted). Stir mixture until chocolate is completely melted. Add the graham cracker crumbs; mix well. Transfer crumb mixture to prepared pan. Press firmly into bottom of pan with a large square of wax paper. Refrigerate until ready to use.

◆ In a large microwavable bowl microwave the water and remaining 5 table-spoons butter on high 1 minute or until butter is melted. Whisk in dry pudding mix; continue to whisk mixture 2 minutes or until completely dissolved. Gradually mix in powdered sugar, stirring until well blended after each addition. Spread over crust. Refrigerate 15 minutes or until firm.

◆ In a medium microwavable bowl microwave the remaining chopped chocolate and heavy cream on high 2 minutes. Stir until chocolate is completely melted

Icebox Bars

and mixture is blended and smooth. Evenly spread and smooth over pudding layer. Refrigerate 2 hours or until set. Use foil lining to remove uncut bars from pan to cutting board. Cut into 24 bars. Store, loosely covered with foil or plastic wrap, in refrigerator. ◆ Makes 24 bars.

Icebox Bars
CHOCOLATE DECADENCE BARS

Coconut Cream Bars

Top off your next summer soiree with these creamy coconut bars.

1¹/₃	cups white chocolate chips, divided use
10	tablespoons butter, divided use
1¹/₂	cups crisp macaroon cookie crumbs
1¹/₃	cups sweetened flake coconut, divided use
¹/₃	cup milk
1	4-serving-size package vanilla flavor instant pudding and pie filling
2	teaspoons coconut-flavored extract
2	cups powdered sugar
¹/₂	cup heavy whipping cream

◆ Line a 9x9x2-inch baking pan with foil (see page 12); lightly spray with nonstick cooking spray. Set aside.

◆ In a large microwavable bowl place half (²/₃ cup) of the white chocolate chips and 5 tablespoons of the butter. Microwave on high for 2 minutes or until butter is melted (chocolate chips will not look completely melted). Stir mixture until white chocolate chips are completely melted. Add the cookie crumbs and ¹/₃ cup coconut; mix well. Transfer crumb mixture to prepared pan. Press firmly into bottom of pan with a large square of wax paper. Refrigerate until ready to use.

◆ In a large microwavable bowl microwave the milk and remaining 5 table-spoons butter on high 1 minute or until butter is melted. Whisk in dry pudding mix and coconut extract; continue to whisk mixture 2 minutes or until completely dissolved. Gradually mix in powdered sugar, stirring until well blended after each addition. Spread over crust. Refrigerate 15 minutes or until firm.

Icebox Bars

◆ Microwave the remaining white chocolate chips and heavy cream in medium microwavable bowl on high 2 minutes. Stir until chocolate chips are completely melted and mixture is blended and smooth. Evenly spread and smooth over pudding layer. Sprinkle with remaining 1 cup coconut, pressing gently into bars. Refrigerate 2 hours or until set. Use foil lining to remove uncut bars from pan to cutting board. Cut into 24 bars. Store, loosely covered with foil or plastic wrap, in refrigerator. ◆ Makes 24 bars.

Icebox Bars
COCONUT CREAM BARS

Peppermint Chocolate Ganache Bars

These dark chocolate bars have just the right amount of peppermint freshness. To crush the candy canes or peppermint candies, place the candies in a heavy, resealable plastic bag. Place the bag on a firm, flat surface and use a rolling pin or mallet to crush the candies into pieces.

2¹/₂	cups finely crushed chocolate wafer or chocolate graham cracker crumbs
¹/₂	cup (1 stick) butter, melted
3	tablespoons sugar
1	cup semisweet chocolate chips
²/₃	cup heavy whipping cream
1	cup powdered sugar
2	8-ounce packages cream cheese, softened
1¹/₂	teaspoons peppermint extract
1	cup frozen non-dairy whipped topping, thawed
²/₃	cup coarsely crushed peppermint candy canes or red hard peppermint candies

◆ Line a 13x9x2-inch baking pan with foil (see page 12); lightly spray with nonstick cooking spray. Set aside.

◆ In a medium bowl combine the cookie crumbs, melted butter, and sugar with a fork or fingers until well blended. Transfer crumb mixture to prepared pan. Press firmly into bottom of pan with a large square of wax paper. Freeze until ready to use.

◆ In a medium saucepan melt the chocolate chips and whipping cream over low heat, stirring occasionally, until smooth. Pour chocolate mixture over crust. Place in freezer at least 10 minutes while preparing the filling.

Icebox Bars

◆ In a large bowl combine the powdered sugar, cream cheese, and peppermint extract. Beat with electric mixer set at low speed, scraping bowl often, until smooth and creamy, about 2–3 minutes. Gently stir in whipped topping. Spread evenly over chocolate ganache layer. Sprinkle with crushed candy, if desired. Cover; freeze 4 hours or overnight. Use foil lining to remove uncut bars from pan to cutting board. Cut into 36 bars. Store, loosely covered with foil or plastic wrap, in refrigerator. ◆ Makes 36 bars.

Black & Tan Espresso Bars

The symphony of chocolate and espresso in these sublime bars is sure to get a standing ovation. For a coffee-lover's gift, pair these grown-up bars with a bag of coffee beans or a gift certificate to the local coffeehouse.

2	cups crushed creme-filled chocolate cookies (e.g., Oreos®)
1/3	cup butter, melted
1/3	cup milk
2	teaspoons unflavored gelatin
2	tablespoons instant espresso or coffee powder
1	14-ounce can sweetened condensed milk, chilled in refrigerator overnight
3/4	cup sour cream

◆ Line an 8x8x2-inch baking pan with foil (see page 12); lightly spray with nonstick cooking spray. Set aside.

◆ In a medium bowl combine the cookie crumbs and melted butter with a fork or fingers until well blended. Transfer crumb mixture to prepared pan. Press firmly into bottom of pan with a large square of wax paper. Freeze until ready to use.

◆ Place the milk in a small saucepan; sprinkle gelatin over (do not stir). Let stand 10 minutes to soften. Add the espresso powder to saucepan and turn the heat under saucepan to medium. Whisk and stir until liquid is very hot (but not boiling) and the gelatin is completely dissolved. Remove from heat and cool 15–20 minutes until lukewarm.

◆ In a medium bowl whisk the chilled sweetened condensed milk and sour cream until blended. Gradually add gelatin mixture, whisking until well blended. Pour and evenly spread over prepared crust. Refrigerate 3 hours or until firm. Use foil lining to remove uncut bars from pan to cutting board. Cut into 24 bars. Store, loosely covered with foil or plastic wrap, in refrigerator. ◆ Makes 24 bars.

Icebox Bars

Index